BAPTISM: *Conscience and Clue for the Church*

BAPTISM:

HOLT, RINEHART AND WINSTON

Conscience and Clue for the Church

WARREN CARR

NEW YORK   CHICAGO   SAN FRANCISCO

Designer: Ernst Reichl
81320-0114
Printed in the United States of America

To Martha and Her Gifts
Ellen, Lynn, Martha Gail, and Debbie

Preface

A preface is necessarily a personal indulgence. As a usual rule, it apparently allows an author the opportunity to explain why he wrote his book, advises the reader on how to read his book, or gives a preview of what is in the book. I dare not venture along any of these trails. The motive for this endeavor defies sufficient particularity to justify its appearance in a preface. I shall be so grateful for those who read it that I will not presume to suggest method or interpretation to them. Finally, I trust that the contents are coherently structured, making a cozy capsule of them superfluous as an introductory note.

I am not willing, however, to forgo completely the luxury of personal indulgence. I do confess that a book on baptism never occurred to me in the earlier days of my ministry. It has come to pass even now as an appropriate part of a wider and more comprehensive concern. One of the persistent frustrations in my pastoral ministry has been the deficiency of lay theology. This unrest has been compounded by my lack of confidence in ordinary corrective endeavors. Theologically oriented sermons, a more vigorous program of Christian education, and emphasis upon study groups for laymen are sound and somewhat effective means for the doctrinal education of the laity, but they are not enough. Immunized to sermons, impervious to Sunday-school lessons, and conspicuously absent from study groups, the average layman absorbs his theological understanding by his participation in the life of the religious institution. He assumes a doctrinal position as a result of what he does in the structure and program of the Church. It is obvious that this milieu is almost void of any theology whatsoever.

Our seminaries and divinity schools have done little to remedy this situation. The research theologian on almost any faculty sometimes gives the impression that he would be disappointed if his theological gems were to be reduced by "pastoral mechanics" to the methodology of practical Christianity. At the same time, the faculty committed to the teaching of pastoral theology seems alternately intimidated by doctrine and disinterested when it gives little or no pragmatic promise. This has left its mark upon the churches. It is generally understood that theologically oriented churches are impractical, while the practical churches are nontheological.

Since the manuscript was finished before this preface, I cannot say, with assured specificity, why I wrote the book. It now seems to me that baptism is not only a worthy concern by itself, but it also affords one of the clearest views into the larger problem before the churches. It is hard to conceive of a greater discrepancy than that existing between baptismal doctrines and baptismal practices in all divisions of the Church. Perhaps, to a very small degree, the book may serve a twofold purpose.

In his first venture, a writer is tempted to include everyone in his acknowledgments. I succumb to that temptation gladly. Friends and colleagues, now lost sight of, have surely contributed to my faith and thought. Former congregations are still very much a part of me. More particularly, I express gratitude to the Reverend Mr. Julius Corpening for both technical and doctrinal criticism. Mrs. C. C. Nelson, Jr., did more than merely type the manuscript. I cannot exaggerate my good fortune in being privileged to use the library facilities of Duke University. The staff of the Divinity School library was particularly gracious, and facilitated my research.

Had it not been for the encouragement and insistence of W. Wesley Shrader, a friend and colleague of many years, I would never have presumed to write anything. My debt to him is enormous. Finally, no busy pastor could ever finish a book of this kind without the understanding and support of the congregation which he serves. The members of the Watts Street Baptist Church not only have spurred me on in this task but are of a kind who do this with full knowledge that many of them do not agree with much of its contents. No minister could hope for more.

WARREN CARR

Durham, North Carolina
April, 1963

Contents

BAPTISM: *Conscience and Clue for the Church*

Chapter One

THE CONSCIENCE

AND THE CLUE

Listen to Luther!

"Blessed be God and the Father of our Lord Jesus Christ, Who according to the riches of His mercy hath preserved in His Church this sacrament at least, untouched and untainted by the ordinances of men, and hath made it free unto all nations and every estate of mankind, nor suffered it to be oppressed by the filthy and godless monsters of greed and superstition. For he desired that by it little children, incapable of greed and superstition, might be initiated and sanctified in the simple faith of His Word; for whom, even today, baptism has its chief blessing." [1]

It is hard to take this statement seriously, even from a man of Luther's stature. His naïveté about little children might be rationalized by the celibate nature of his earlier years, but his assumption regarding the invulnerability of baptism is another question. The Reformer sometimes described baptism as a ship on the sea. Ironically enough, he provoked one of the greatest doctrinal tempests ever to "rock the boat." When Luther found himself in the center of the storm, and lifted his hand to steady the ship, he brought more chaos and disorder to the very situation he wanted to control. And his "ship of baptism" on the choppy waters of the Reformation was

[1] Martin Luther, *Three Treatises* (Philadelphia: Muhlenberg Press, 1943), p. 168.

further impeded as Luther shifted his weight indiscriminately from one side to the other.

Martin Luther was primarily a polemicist. Neither his theology in general nor his theology of baptism is to be understood apart from this role. He contended within the Church more than he debated with the world outside the Church. The question of baptism was perennially in focus. Not only was baptism touched and tainted by men, but Martin Luther contributed his share to the process. When he was fighting with Rome, his chief weapon was "justification by faith." Man's salvation, he declared, was not in the hands of the Church or any of its officials. The grace of God was the hope of man's redemption. At the same time, the doctrine of justification by faith highlighted man's individual and personal response of faith to God's redemptive and gracious act. This accent upon faith and the subjective responsibility of the believer prompted some of Luther's contemporaries to doubt the necessity or even the importance of infant baptism. It is common knowledge that Zwingli thought, during his earlier years at Zurich, that baptism could be deferred, to the advantage of both the individual and the Church, until the years of discretion.

It is evident that Luther never meant his doctrine to be so interpreted. While he was preoccupied in his struggle with Rome, others were gathering in the theological bush to oppose him. Poorly organized and armed with nondescript theological weapons, nevertheless they attacked Luther with immediate and devastating results. They accused him of toying with the Reformation movement; to their view he was not willing to follow it to its logical conclusion. The kind of faith and commitment which Luther had called for could mean nothing less or different in their eyes than a church of regenerate and responsible members who had been called out from the world. These liberals of the Reformation were not to be content until the Church had become separated from either or both the world and the State. Luther, however, could not tolerate such religious extremity. As he turned to do battle with these new and unexpected enemies, he seized an old weapon—that of infant baptism. Luther spoke, in this context, of the objectivity of salvation. The accent was upon grace, even to the exclusion of personal faith.

Luther cannot be singled out in this respect. He was neither the first nor the last to misuse the doctrine and practice of baptism when expediency demanded. Baptism has been subjected to a process of accommodation ever since its inception as an act of the Church. It can and will be documented that the majority of church leaders, both past and present, have used baptism to suit their particular purpose. This practice, virtually unchallenged until now, serves to explain the evident baptismal malaise fitfully plaguing the Church.

1 Conscience

The story of Christian baptism is not a pleasant one. No other act in the Church's life has been the victim of the same degree of pragmatic utilitarianism. Each institutional segment seems to have used it as a means to its own ends. To its surprise, the Church early discovered that baptism, acting as a painful conscience, resisted its exploitative treatment. Responding with alacrity, baptism appears to have been the persistent reminder of what constituted both the nature and the mission of the Christian community. In turn, the Church sought relief from its pangs of conscience by bringing incredible pressure to bear upon the integrity of baptism. This has been so because the rite of baptism has not lent itself to the Church's desire to assure its position in the world. In the long run, however, the conscience of the Church has been crippled and can no longer perform its function with its customary vigor.

The analogy of baptism and conscience is rendered meaningful because baptism has always been the act of Christian initiation; it can never, even in liberal views, be completely divorced from the incorporation of a person into the life of the Church. It is the first determinant of the nature of membership in the Church. The manner by which the Church enlists or incorporates its members will have appreciable bearing upon the quality of its life. For all communions of the Church, the memory of the time of baptism, by the parents, in one tradition, and by the baptized themselves, in the

other, has been important to one's life as a Christian. The emotional tone, the quality of sincerity, the clarity of explanation, and
the effectiveness of the symbol of baptism are not to be dismissed
from the act of Christian initiation. The more vivid are these elements in recall, the more meaningful they are thought to have been.

Baptism, at the outset, was involved in the relationship of the
Church and the world. It was a door, swinging inwardly, through
which the convert came from the world to the Church. Presumably
he left a life of faithlessness for one of faith. Baptism opened on a
new life and shut upon an old one. Such an exalted view of baptism
belonged to the Church in its missionary stage, before it had fully
recognized the exigencies implicit in becoming a social institution.
The believing community had gathered through the rite of baptism
and awaited the early return of the risen Lord.

What lay behind this high indifference to the world and all its
eternal structures? . . . In larger part . . . the answer lies in the
Christian's underlying world view of history in its plan of beginning
and end.

The Christian interpreted from Judaism a conception of the
scheme of history radically different from the classical Greek
theory, which was the cyclical view that history moves in eternal
recurrence, around and around, with no beginning or end. The
Hebrew-Christian view, on the other hand, conceived of history
as the fulfillment of a divine plan, a single line moving from a
point in time when God's creation began, through the crisis or
central point in time when God revealed himself in Christ, to the
finis when God would ring the curtain down on history and end
the present-world order in a mighty act of judgment.[2]

Beach and Niebuhr expand upon the foregoing idea by reminding
us that the ethical concern of the early church was influenced by a
vivid eschatology. That concern motivated the Christian to be a
self-conscious part of a community which was separated from the

[2] Waldo Beach and H. Richard Niebuhr, *Christian Ethics* (New York: The
Ronald Press Company, 1955), pp. 49-50.

world and had little traffic with it. "The faith that the Christ had come," say the authors, "and the hope that Christ would come again, closing the world order, account in part for the indifference of the Christian to the social structures of the world. Since the whole machinery of life, economic, racial, political, and domestic, was soon to be swept away, why put one's hope in them or struggle to change them?" [3]

As time passed and the coming of the Lord did not eventuate, the early Church realized that it needed to maintain itself as one of the world's institutions. It was soon involved with sustaining an ethical impact upon the world, while accommodating to it. In a milieu of alternating hostility and indifference, the Church found that making friends with the world was no easy task. Only after it became both respectable and strong did society afford it a friendlier environment. A logical course was followed to that welcome end. Poorly prepared in structure and method for those days, the Church borrowed the tools with which society established and sustained its many secular institutions. It then required the right kind of people to employ such secular instruments. This could be accomplished in but one way. The world's "skilled labor"—skilled in all but the Christian faith—had to be put to work in the Church.

These secular artisans came through the door of baptism. The Church cleverly invented a double hinge for its baptismal door. It no longer shut the convert off from the world. He could walk through the door both ways. People came and went through the door of baptism in such numbers that no one knew where the world ended and the Church began. This was not altogether undesirable. It was the only means by which the Church could have any real impact upon the culture in which it lived. But while the Church ethically sensitized the world, the world secularized the Church. Baptism was a busy and undiscriminating entrance. We can be grateful that the double hinge developed a creak of protest, that, indeed, baptism continues to make a noise like a conscience.

A recent novel inadvertently suggests the latest function of baptism, consequent to the merger of the secular and the sacred. "A

[3] *Ibid.,* p. 50.

daily baptism in hot water gave a man the illusion, if not of renewed innocence, at least of renewed competence in his traffic with
the world. Scrubby genius was always at a discount. The biggest
killings were made by men with fresh collars and clean hands." [4]
If it is true that the Church is now more concerned with competence
to do traffic with the world than with innocence in the world, a
second switch is also necessary. It must trade "clean hands and a
pure heart" for "clean hands and a fresh collar."

If the analogy appears unnecessarily harsh, the report of a study
in *Newsweek* helps support it. The study was the project of The
American Institute of Management. The Roman Catholic Church and
the American Telephone and Telegraph Company are deemed com-
parable because "both are huge and well organized, pursue strong
fiscal policies, and are extremely well managed." The story continues:

> Big Business and Big Church may seem an unlikely twosome,
> but the institute thinks otherwise. For the past seven years, while
> making management audits for such business empires as AT&T,
> Humble Oil, and Proctor & Gamble, the organization has also
> been studying the way the Vatican runs the Roman Catholic
> Church. . . .
>
> Assuming the church should be run as though it were General
> Motors, the AIM said that under Pope John XXIII the Vatican
> has improved so much from a viewpoint of "management excel-
> lence" it now rates a score of 9,010 on the AIM evaluation table.
> Not bad, and nearly as impressive as the AT&T score—9,520
> of an optimum 10,000.[5]

Lest anyone infer that this is a criticism of the Roman Catholic
Church alone, the author hastens to observe that he belongs to a
denomination whose greatest concern would be whether it could
match the Roman Catholic score. This circumstance belongs neither

---

[4] Morris L. West, *Backlash* (New York: William Morrow & Co., Inc.,
1958), p. 75.
[5] *Newsweek*, LX (September 3, 1962), 47.

to the Roman Catholic Church nor to Southern Baptists alone. A case in point is the action of a Presbyterian church in North Carolina. It was debating whether to remain in a present downtown location, to relocate, or to colonize. After considerable controversy and unrest, the church eventually sought the counsel of an IBM computer. At this writing it has not yet been determined whether the Holy Spirit spoke to the church through or for the computer.

However much baptism may have been a free-swinging dual-action door making for easy passage between the Church and the world, it was something different within the Church. The Reformation's gains were marred by a complication which has persisted until the present. Religious pluralism or denominationalism was conceived in the Reformation. The secular onslaught from the outside and the growing division within created manifold problems for the Church. These problems were reflected in the rite of baptism. While it continued to prove less and less a line of demarcation between the Church and the world, baptism became a higher and more formidable barrier between the inner compartments of the Church. It is now obvious that the most heated discussions about baptism stem from division within the Church, rather than from division between the Church and the secular order.

The use of baptism as a means of distinguishing one Christian from another, one church from another, remains a sorry and perplexing spectacle. It is often lamented that it is easier now to join the Church, whether by infant or believers' baptism, than it is to join practically any other contemporary social institution. This is true only if we are talking of joining the Church from the world. If one wishes, however, to transfer from one denomination of the Church to another, he will encounter a maximum of difficulty. Continuing the analogy of baptism as a door, one further illustration may be useful. The Church is now like a suite of offices connected with the outside world by a single entrance. This main door to the Church is marked: WELCOME—ENTER WITHOUT KNOCKING. The doors connecting the various offices within the larger complex are not as inviting. They are marked: PRIVATE—CHECK WITH THE RECEPTIONIST.

This twofold misuse of baptism is a scandal; indeed, greater exploitation of the rite is hardly conceivable. However, there is another which is more serious than this. What happens to baptism within each private room of the complex of the Church is of major consequence. In fact, the exploitation of baptism in the Church's traffic with the world and the exploitation of baptism by the Church's divisions are not likely to be remedied until some treatment is given to the situation existing within the divisions themselves. This is more significant than each of the other distortions.

The Church Ecumenical and the Church Divided have this much in common. Baptism has been distorted at the most sensitive points of the Church's mission and ministry; an example is the incongruity between infant baptism and evangelism—a fact which will be developed later on. Meanwhile, it is fair to say that paedobaptists have been both ludicrous and evasive in their attempts to disclaim the obvious antipathy between the two. Infant baptism is an embarrassment to the established church whenever it goes forth to evangelize the world. Its attempts to avoid this embarrassment by the distortion of its own doctrine of baptism are more harmful than would be its bearing up under ridicule. On the other hand, believers' baptism, whenever its doctrine is taken seriously, is irreconcilable in both content and method with the main stream of Christian education. It will become apparent that the churches of this tradition also make their baptism mean whatever is convenient at a given time.

Other distortions of the role of baptism come to light when it becomes inexpedient for baptism to enjoy its rightful place in worship. We shall see that the two traditions in question resort to private baptisms, family rites, and similar evasions if it seems prudent to do so. Baptism's relationship to the ecumenical objectives is rendered ambivalent to say the least. Generally speaking, if it promises to be helpful in achieving ecumenical goals, the leaders of the movement endeavor to make baptism a central factor in their discussions. If baptism promises to be a barrier, the leaders seek to shunt it to the side. This pattern prevails more among American church leaders than those of England and Europe.

The question of ecumenicity is not to be confined to that of doctrine. Baptism, in its original integrity, passes a strong judgment upon the class and racial exclusiveness which characterizes the Church of the times. It is ironical that in the Church's preoccupation with these sins and attempts to abolish them, little recourse to baptism and its meaning has come to the fore. Were Paul to stand in the midst of our cultural crisis, he would surely say: "For just as the body is one and has many members, and all the members of the body, though many, are one body, so it is with Christ. For by one Spirit we were all baptized into one body—Jews or Greeks, slaves or free —and all were made to drink of one Spirit." [6]

The moral and ethical implications of the rite have not been emphasized in contemporary religious discussion. The absence of the ethical note can only mean that baptism has suffered distortion in this respect as well. The Church cannot compromise its moral stance without making some adjustment in baptism as to faith and practice. Baptism involves social and personal morality at one and the same time. A rakish demeanor regarding individual morality while plunging into the vast social questions of the day does not escape the notice of the conscience of baptism. In the midst of modern tolerance, even the Church is losing the capacity for being shocked. The moral ethic, beset by obscurantist deviations and lost beneath a confusion of excuses, continues to emerge with renewed vigor from the waters of baptism. The act still occupies itself with the old words of sin and death. "Do you not know," wrote the apostle Paul to the Romans, "that all of us who have been baptized into Christ Jesus were baptized into his death? . . . We know that our old self was crucified with him so that the sinful body might be destroyed, and we might no longer be enslaved to sin. For he who has died is freed from sin. . . . So you also must consider your-selves dead to sin and alive to God in Christ Jesus." [7]

Although the significance of baptism is being strongly emphasized in these introductory notes, I do not believe that the matter is being overdone. There is no better insight into the manner by which the Church reveals its self-esteem than in its relationship to the "sacra-

[6] I Cor. 12:12-13.
[7] Rom. 6:3, 6, 7, 11.

ments." The distinguished English Baptist, H. Wheeler Robinson, is clear at this point: "The idea of the Church is revealed in her idea of the sacraments. If she thinks little or nothing of them how can she think much of herself, seeing that these are characteristic acts of the ecclesia? But if she thinks much of that which they concentrate and express, for what should she contend more earnestly than for a worthy interpretation of them?" [8]

The Church has practiced to the contrary. Instead of seeking a worthy interpretation of the "sacrament" of baptism it has been guilty of distortion, confusion, and reductionism. The misfortune of this distortion is further compounded because the Church persists in its reluctance to face up to this fact. However, one noteworthy exception to this evasive pattern does exist. Whenever the question of authenticity arises between believers' baptism and infant baptism, the opposing Churches aim their heaviest doctrinal artillery at one another. For the most part, though, the Church tends to skirt the issue of baptism if at all possible. Having made the act an unwilling ally in its conspiracy with the world, little enthusiasm is in evidence for redressing the wrongful use of baptism.

Let us hope that the Church will not succeed in its attempt to evade or suppress the whole question of baptism. If it is to recover some of its essential qualities, it needs to hear the cry of the sensitive and disturbed conscience.

2   Dealing With a Troublesome Conscience

"Conscience is the indicator of the measure of agreement between our conduct and our values, whatever they may be." [9] As the conscience of the Church, baptism may serve as the measure of agreement between its theology and practice, its faith and work. By the same token, whether or not the Church really wishes to recover its original integrity will probably be made clear in the baptismal waters. There is always reason for suspicion whenever baptism is ignored or

[8] H. Wheeler Robinson, *The Christian Experience of the Holy Spirit* (New York and London: Harper & Row, Publishers, 1928), p. 184.

[9] Gordon Allport, *The Individual and His Religion* (New York: The Macmillan Company, 1950), p. 91.

purposely set aside in the processes of the Church's self-inventory.

A committee which dealt in part with baptism for the North American Conference on Faith and Order dispatched the matter with noticeable abruptness. Meeting at Oberlin College, Ohio, in September, 1957, the committee had this to say about baptism:

> . . . our varying and sometimes conflicting understanding of the meaning and the nature of baptism reflects our difference with respect to the Church, its authority and order, the requirements for membership in it, the nature and place of its sacraments or ordinances, the agencies and organs of its continuing historic life in the world, and the means used by the Holy Spirit to sanctify its members. These and like differences profoundly affect our understanding of baptism and seem to make it unlikely that a study of baptism alone will offer any final guide in our search for unity.[10]

The committee's conclusion is hard to understand. The report describes baptism as if it were a mirror reflecting the basic differences which keep the Church from its ecumenical fulfillment. The committee then turns the mirror to the wall, apparently hoping for the achievement of Christian unity by concealing the causes which divide the Church.

This is not the first time that zeal for ecumenicity has pushed baptism to the side. The committee enjoyed ample precedent. Charles Clayton Morrison, although by no means the most orthodox voice among the Disciples of Christ, speaks with evident authority and is heard with respect. He belongs to a tradition in which baptism has occupied a prominent place from the beginning. Morrison's concern for the unity of Christianity prompted him to undertake an unwelcome chore; he felt obliged to write a book on baptism. The book came close to holding the rite in contempt. The author's tone is apologetic and condescending. "It is with great reluctance," he explained, "that the author has gained the consent of his own mind to write this book and to send it forth. In a time when men's souls

---

[10] Paul Minear (ed.), *The Nature of the Unity We Seek* (St. Louis, Mo.: The Bethany Press, 1958), p. 198.

are vibrating to problems involving the most vital interests and ideals of humanity, one's prestige is not likely to be enhanced by connecting one's name with a book on *The Meaning of Baptism*. It will seem like turning from the living present to the dead past to discuss this question again." [11]

In that dead past a man like Alexander Campbell was known to have debated the question of baptism for more than a week without skipping a day. It would have been better if Morrison had stayed his pen. Baptism was compromised by his technique of reductionism.

In the light of the preceding examples, a passion for ecumenicity could logically be expected to discount the significance of baptism. One appears to be the inevitable consequence of the other. If so, Southern Baptists, who do not officially sound the trumpets for Christian unity, should prove the point. Since they often employ their great and sprawling strength as a boon to denominational isolationism, it ought to follow that they focus their theological life upon baptism as a matter of central concern. The casual Baptist and the casual onlooker assume that this is so. This is an unwarranted assumption.

E. Y. Mullins, president of the Southern Baptist Theological Seminary for almost forty years, was a notable example of a theologian who neglected the question of baptism. As prolific in his writings as any other leading Southern Baptist figure, he stood in the center of his tradition in regard to the ecumenical question. In an article printed in a Baptist periodical of May 9, 1914, called "The Standard," Mullins echoed the sentiment of most of his colleagues: "As I see the matter the open membership plea proceeds on the assumption that all denominationalism is wrong, those of Baptists as well as others. . . . It is infinitely better for the world that Christians embody their convictions in distinct organizations, love each other and cooperate in all practicable ways, than that our Christianity should become so colorless and our motives so feeble that we would be without vitality enough to differ." This reveals a trend away from a more mellow attitude in former years. Some six

[11] Charles Clayton Morrison, *The Meaning of Baptism* (Chicago: Disciples Publication Society, 1914), p. 5.

years before, he had explained, ". . . Baptists have not been particularly active as a rule in efforts toward organic Christian union. They are not indeed without profound interest in the matter. But being unable to surrender any element of their simple church order without fatally weakening it, and being unwilling to urge others to violate their consciences, they have awaited the leading of Providence rather than sought to reorganize Christianity." [12]

As Mullins moved ever closer to denominational isolation, it logically follows that he would have become more involved with the question of baptism. On the contrary, Mullins never showed any great interest in the subject. He did attack infant baptism and its implications with telling vigor. But a positive theology of his own on the subject did not appear. Sydney Ahlstrom, writing on "Theology in America," shows his surprise that Mullins revealed a "relative disinterest in questions of the church itself, its ministry, and its 'ordinances.' In his major doctrinal treatise, even a matter so distinctive in his tradition as baptism does not receive a full page of discussion." [13] This fact is doubly surprising because the book to which Ahlstrom refers, *The Christian Religion in its Doctrinal Expression*, was written primarily for use as a textbook or student manual.

It has been suggested that Mullins was so sure of his position on baptism that he hardly thought it worth the trouble to defend it. This would reflect on him as a theologian. Theologians, who are certain of the divinity of Jesus, go to great lengths in order to put the doctrine in substantial and acceptable form. It is more likely that Mullins, like many others, found it easier and more exciting to argue about proper baptism, infant or believers', than to engage the subject of baptism itself. Again one suspects that the relegation of baptism to a position of unimportance in Christian tradition is not a coincidence. The studied indifference to baptism by the scholar fits

[12] E. Y. Mullins, *The Axioms of Religion* (Philadelphia: American Baptist Publication Society, 1908), p. 231.
[13] Smith and Jamison (eds.), *The Shaping of American Religions* (Princeton, N.J.: Princeton University Press, 1961), Vol. I, chap. 5, "Theology in America," by Sydney Ahlstrom, p. 307.

too neatly into a general pattern of keeping the question as quiet as possible.

Suppression is not without its dangers. F. W. Dillistone effectively warns against the evident and persisting suppression of baptism by the Church. He begins with the reminder that water baptism is one of the commonest forms of symbolic activity in the religious history of mankind. It relates primarily to man's desire for the intensifying or renewing of life. Water from the heavens has been thought to possess life-giving properties. To be sprinkled with water was to have life renewed. Water gushing out of the ground, symbolically understood, came from the womb of the Earth Mother. Immersion in this water procured the gift of immortality in ancient mythology. To descend into still water is to return to the source of creativity. Water has also connoted a dark and foreboding threat. As surely as the Red Sea separated Israel from Canaan, water stands between man and the land of promise. In some mythical imagery, Christ is the One who has descended into the waters and destroyed the monsters of the deep.[14]

Dillistone makes use of an illustration offered by Erich Fromm to suggest that these symbols do not belong entirely to the dimension of immediate realization. As often as not, they are part of the subconscious life of man. A patient of Fromm's had dreamed of a beautiful city on top of a hill. There was a river dividing the city and the person. "I feel that if I can only cross the river everything will be all right," the patient explained. "It was an ordinary river, in fact like the river in our town I was always a little afraid of as a child." Fromm observes that "this is one of those important dreams in which a decisive step away from mental illness is taken. . . . To be sure, the patient is not yet well, but he has experienced the most important thing short of being well, a clear and vivid vision of life in which he is not a haunted criminal, but a free person. He also visualized that, in order to get there, he must cross a river, an old and universally-used symbol of an important decision, or starting

---

[14] F. W. Dillistone, *Christianity and Symbolism* (Philadelphia: The Westminster Press, 1955), pp. 183-193.

a new form of existence—birth or death—of giving up one form of life for another." [15]

The Church must also cross its river. Among its most important decisions is whether to allow the waters of baptism to keep it forever removed from its original nature. Dillistone is convinced that water and new life is a symbol which the Church may ignore only at great risk.

In part, here is his trenchant warning:

> In the more sophisticated life of modern time, these realistic images are in eclipse and the mythic associations of the baptismal water have retreated farther and farther into the background. The font usually occupies an inconspicuous position in the Church and the use of water is highly artificial. It may, indeed, be held that it is better to have no connections with the realms of mystery and darkness, and that all primordial images of the life-giving and regenerating properties of water should be rigorously excluded from the Christian sacramental system. But the power of these archetypal images is too great to be rendered null and void by any process of deliberate exclusion. *If they are not sanctified within a Christian context they will almost certainly present themselves in demonic forms* [my italics]. To find a way of allowing Baptism to exercise its power within the Christian community at the deepest level of the human psyche is one of the most urgent tasks of our day.[16]

Those demonic forms, of which Dillistone speaks, need not be the hydra-headed monsters of ancient Greek mythology. Some modern forms, while not as spectacular, may prove even more difficult to uproot and destroy.

One such form is a chameleonic type of baptism giving rise to constant theological confusion about the rite. Making baptism mean

[15] Erich Fromm, *The Forgotten Language* (New York: Holt, Rinehart and Winston, Inc., 1951), pp. 154-155.

[16] Dillistone, *op. cit.*, p. 187.

whatever the situation demands infects it with a demonic quality. "Among many Christian groups baptismal practice is in confusion because baptismal theology is so indefinite or, in some cases, faulty," is the opinion of T. C. Smith. "Very little emphasis," he continues, "has been placed . . . on the meaning of baptism for those who submit to it." [17] The minister in parish and congregation will recognize that Smith's criticism is based on fact. He has been conditioned by seminary training and his parish experience to give little or no attention to a doctrinal explanation of baptism. It may be provided upon request. If no request is forthcoming, the church administering the baptism is likely to make no mention of it at all.

Baptism, as a device for dividing the Church, must plead guilty to demonic possession. Argument over this aspect of baptism goes on unabated. The author confesses that he hears little or nothing about baptism in his own Baptist denomination, until the question of receiving members from other communions is raised. Much controversy, both heated and prolonged, is then generated. The books we read about baptism are primarily concerned with the argument between infant baptism and believers' baptism. The centrality of Christian baptism is not able to command a proportionate degree of interest or scholarship.

In modern dress, baptism parades on the religious stage to a variety of commentary. Its appearance is met with a "babel of tongues." Its contemporary demonic forms are covered with words: "Baptism never saved anybody." "Baptism is only a symbol." "Infant baptism has nothing to do with the infant, it gives parents a chance to rededicate their lives." "Whether infant baptism means anything or not, it certainly is a sweet service and means so much to the parents." The demonic often sounds both innocuous and sweet; it is neither.

[17] Duke McCall (ed.), *What Is the Church?* (Nashville, Tenn.: Broadman Press, 1958), chap. 4, "The Doctrine of Baptism in the New Testament," by T. C. Smith, p. 64.

3   Renewed Interest in Baptism in Europe

There is another side to the picture. A revival of interest in and concern for the rite of baptism has become focalized in Continental Europe and in England. In contrast to the United States, the leading scholars abroad are bringing their theological acumen to bear upon the question of baptism. It gives some hope that the Church everywhere will return to an appreciation of the central importance of the rite and renew it with doctrinal vitality.

An inadvertent but decisive commentary upon the American position may be found in the statement of a committee which met in Edinburgh in 1960. It was part of a Faith and Order Conference such as the one held at Oberlin, to which reference has been made. The contrast between the position of the doctrinal committee at Edinburgh and the one at Oberlin is most striking. A portion of the Edinburgh reports is as follows: "It must be admitted in all honesty that holy baptism, upon which the New Testament places so much emphasis, has been very greatly neglected by the church and individual Christians of all confessions."

At the same time the question of baptism has long since occupied a prominent place in ecumenical discussion, and the spectacular revival of interest in the subject of Christian initiation in some circles (particularly but not exclusively in the churches of the Reformed and Anglican traditions) has made it increasingly clear that baptism is not only important in itself, but also closely related to the broader questions of the unity of the Church.[18]

Unlike the American committee, this group decided against turning the giant mirror of baptism to the wall. It agreed that the reflection of the Church's manifold problems in the search for unity must be viewed in the clear and distinctive setting of baptism. These words are heartening; they strike the appropriate note of relevance. As such

[18] G. H. W. Lampe, and David M. Paton (eds.), *One Lord, One Baptism* (London: S.C.M. [Student Christian Movement] Press, 1960), p. 45.

they will bear more fruit in the ecumenical vineyard than will be the
case with the recommendations of the North American committee.
The Edinburgh conference did not confine its appraisal only to the
ecumenical question. It went on to say, and happily so:

> Since baptism encompasses the whole Christian life, lack of
> clarity concerning the meaning of baptism leads to uncertainty all
> along the line. It is beyond dispute that in no church body does
> baptism have the decisive significance which the witness of the
> New Testament ascribes to it. Here we all have much to learn.
> A serious penetration into the meaning of baptism and an appro-
> priation of the treasure given in baptism would give preaching
> and teaching both a centrally focused content and a new breadth,
> together with an insight which clarifies and unifies the whole of
> Christian life. The more the baptised learn to see their whole
> life in the light of their baptism, the more does their life take
> on the pattern of life "in Christ." It is also of decisive importance
> to pastoral care to say to a troubled human being, "You are
> baptised," with all the assurance which this implies.[19]

One need not agree with every theological implication in the foregoing statement in order to appreciate its central thrust. The committee at Edinburgh is agreed that baptism should not be ignored
but ought to be used positively because of its bearing upon all the
essential elements of the Church. It is still too early to tell which of
the two ecumenical committees will have greater influence upon the
Church. Obviously, a vote is here cast for the committee at Edinburgh. But if the Church should follow this lead, it must make sure
that something more than another expedient course is being followed; renewed concern for baptism must be marked by theological
depth and ethical sensitivity. Lacking such seriousness, not renewal,
but accelerated obsolescence could well result. Raising a hue and cry
for the renewal of baptism's importance only to disallow its real
meaning would be tragic. The rite would become a victim of what
Helmut Thielicke calls a "ciphered nihilism," a disguised or covert

[19] *Ibid.,* p. 70.

nothingness. "Every philosophy," observed Thielicke, "created by making an absolute out of a relative can maintain itself only for a short time before it succumbs to the opposing forces which it has itself provoked. In this sense the history of modern thought with its succession of 'isms' is like a gigantic parade of idols. And how comical the idols that have just marched past look from behind." [20] Enough of these comic forms of baptism have already gone by; let us hope that we have seen the last of their kind.

Without the proper elements in breadth and depth, the revival of baptism can have no more permanent effect than a jet trail; first it marks the sky with its high line, lofty, straight, and clean; then fuzziness; and finally it is not visible at all, as if an impatient teacher had erased its meaningless scrawl from the atmospheric board.

4   Keeping Baptism in Perspective

The recovery of baptism demands proper perspective. Balance is essential, for the case for baptism may be argued to the extent of the ridiculous.

"In the study of baptism it is necessary to guard against two extreme positions. The importance of baptism must not be magnified beyond a point warranted by New Testament teaching, and equal care must be given not to minimize the importance of the rite to the extent that it becomes a symbol stripped of all meaning." [21]

At least two steps are necessary to a desirable balance. First of all, in carrying through our analogy between baptism and conscience, the place of compromise and casuistry must be determined. Secondly, the integrity of the symbol of baptism must be defended. The correlation between baptismal theology and practice is very much a part of this second consideration.

Rightly placed, casuistry can prevent undue emphasis upon baptism. Nothing could be worse than to enclose the Church in a bap-

---

[20] Helmut Thielicke, *Nihilism,* trans. John Doberstein (New York: Harper & Row, Publishers, 1961), p. 21.

[21] Duke McCall (ed.), *What Is the Church?* (Nashville, Tenn.: Broadman Press, 1958), chap. 4, "The Doctrine of Baptism in the New Testament," by T. C. Smith, p. 65.

tismal strait jacket. It should not be made the prisoner of any dogma. Casuistry and compromise in themselves are not improper means by which the Church may deal with its baptismal conscience. Conscience and casuistry are not enemies; they are necessary to each other. Without casuistry, conscience runs the risk of irrelevance. Without conscience, casuistry loses its reason for existence.

The close connection of casuistry with conscience should not be overemphasized. Conscience is more than whimsy or caprice. It is basic and universal. "The cultural relativity of conscience is marked," admits Gordon Allport, "but even so, the case may have been overstated by anthropologists. It is a matter calling for more study, particularly today when it is vital to know just how much moral agreement there is among peoples of the world. In spite of differing tabus and imperatives, it seems that all people prize kindness to children, loyalty to the ingroup, and they have a not wholly capricious sense of justice. We cannot be too sure that the content of human conscience is endlessly varied." [22]

The same may be said for the conscience of baptism in particular as is said for conscience in general. Baptism is not merely the invention of man. It is a God-given action and symbol. So far as the Church is concerned, it has basic and universal qualities which ought not to be subject to the pressures of religious societies or the whimsy of churchmen. It may also prove to be more perceptive than is ordinarily realized. The disparity between conduct and conscience is not always the primary or greater disturbance. Conflict between conscience and desire can be equally disturbing.[23] The conflict of the contemporary Church may be similarly perceived. Baptism provides judgmental insight not only into its conduct but also into its basic attitudes.

History reveals, paradoxically enough, some examples of how baptism has been enforced with rigidity and dogmatism. The ag-

[22] Gordon Allport, *The Individual and His Religion* (New York: The Macmillan Company, 1950), p. 65.

[23] Anton Boisen, *Religion in Crisis and Custom* (New York: Harper & Row, Publishers, 1955), p. 194.

gressiveness with which Roman Catholicism assures the legitimate baptism of its offspring is not only indelicate but often offensive. Equally offensive to the true spirit of Christianity is the rigidity found in many churches practicing the baptism of believers. Aged, sick, and indigent persons have been refused full membership in these churches despite the fact that they were physically unable to undergo the rigors of baptism by immersion. Such examples are evidence that the Church, at times, is pathological in its insistence upon the importance of ritually accurate baptism. Specifically, "Conscience becomes pathological when it (a) functions in too rigid or automatic a manner, so that realistic judgment about the outcome of intended actions is disturbed or (b) when the breakdown toward 'panic' occurs and a greater or lesser sense of complete annihilation is experienced instead of a warning signal. . . ." [24]

The shudder of the newly baptized is not always the true emotion of a new life. It may be no more than the neurotic spasm of a dogma-ridden baptism registering its impact upon the life of the convert. This extreme usually connotes the lack of real assurance about baptism. It may represent the Church's endeavor to rid itself of ecclesiastical guilt feelings. As has been suggested before, this would appear to be the case when the divisions of the Church argue so vigorously with each other on the question of baptism.

A relevant Church will employ some compromise. It is beyond doubt that baptism has been subjected to compromise throughout the life of the Church. In itself this constitutes no tragedy at all. The problem arises when the Church attempts to conceal the compromises which it has made. Its endeavor to present the compromised position on baptism as the normal and right position is hypocritical to say the least. Casuistry is always confessional. What Reinhold Niebuhr said about the sins of men is applicable to the Church in this instance: "No man, however deeply involved in sin, is able to regard the misery of sin as normal. Some memory of a previous condition of blessedness seems to linger in his soul; some

[24] Otto Fenichel, *The Psychoanalytic Theory of Neurosis* (New York: W. W. Norton & Company, Inc., 1945), p. 136.

echo of the law which he has violated seems to resound in his conscience. Every effort to give the habits of sin the appearance of normality betrays something of the frenzy of an uneasy conscience." [25]

The Church has refused to declare the abnormality of its baptismal adjustments. It has not confessed to the practice of casuistry. Surely some modifications had to be made, and it is good that the Church had the courage to act accordingly. But it is not good that the Church has tried to obscure its compromising tactic. It is better for the adjustments to be seen in the light of their circumstances. Had the Church been willing to do this, the points of its departure from right thought and practice could be more easily discerned. This would mean in turn that a remedy could be more quickly and easily found. To conceal compromise is to blot out the trail over which it has traveled. The way back is then hard to find.

A confessional casuistry will make sure that baptism is not given an exaggerated place in the life of the Church. Perspective and balance demand that it not be entirely negated. Much of the answer to this need may be found in maintaining the integrity of its symbol. Casuistry must never be allowed to destroy either the reality of the baptismal symbol or the reality of that which is symbolized. No symbol keeps its integrity if the reality it represents is subject to constant change. By the same token, the reality behind the symbol must find its expression in the symbol that represents it. It cannot convey its meaning through an unlimited and arbitrarily selected number of symbols.

If a symbol is to represent a reality other than itself, it must possess a reality of its own. It does not point to the other reality as does a sign. In fact, man does not conceive the reality behind the symbol as much as he does the reality of the symbol itself. What is conceived in the symbol therefore must be true to the reality which has brought it into being. A symbol is not a cover which conceals reality; instead, it expresses its mystery. One does not "go" at a symbol as a child peels off the top of a box of Cracker-jacks with no

[25] Reinhold Niebuhr, *The Nature and Destiny of Man* (New York: Charles Scribner's Sons, 1949), Part I, p. 265.

idea of what "hidden treasure" lies within. Unless the ultimate reality is commensurate with its representing symbol, both the reality and the symbol lose their meaning.

A symbol "is designed to represent a state of affairs. It may do this accurately or inaccurately, vividly or dully, in a complicated or in a simple fashion. But it must represent, at least in some degree, the general pattern of the configuration of which it is a symbol. There is no one-to-one correspondence between symbol and conception, but there are patterns of correspondence which govern the relations between the two and prevent the connection being purely arbitrary and ephemeral." [26]

Early in its history, the Church adopted two forms of baptism, which have persisted until the present. The modification of baptism has not occurred so much in its outward forms as in its interior meaning. Consequently, both infant baptism and believers' baptism have remained as forms. That they have appeared to mean what they no longer mean either to the Church as a whole or to the divisions of the Church that brought them into being is sheer mockery.

This raises another question. Correlation between the practice and theology of the rite of baptism is absolutely necessary. The practice of baptism must not continue with either an obscure theology or no theology. When separated from its original doctrine, religious practice often devises a new dogma to justify its own structure and operation. It is not uncommon for a new theology stemming from a familiar religious practice to contradict the doctrine that gave birth to that practice in its initial form.

A Presbyterian note of alarm is germane to the Church as a whole. Lewis Schenck claims that no rubric defined in the Confession of the Reformed Churches has received less attention and is less understood than that of baptism.[27] An English Baptist, Neville Clarke, is too quick to agree. He caustically observes, "From the earliest

---

[26] F. W. Dillistone, *Christianity and Symbolism* (Philadelphia: The Westminster Press, 1955), p. 25.

[27] Lewis Bevens Schenck. *The Presbyterian Doctrine of Children in the Covenant* (New Haven, Conn.: Yale University Press, 1940), p. 155.

times infant baptism has been a practice in search of a theology; in many quarters it is still so today." [28]

Schenck and Clarke make the same mistake. They fail to cover enough ground in their comments. Theological vacuity and consequent distortion are not the characteristics of infant baptism alone. They characterize baptism in general. The thirst for theological meaning is no longer quenched at the baptismal spring. Given no cup of cold water, theology knows itself as an intruder, takes the hint, and quietly steals away. In summary it may be said that baptism will maintain proper balance and perspective so long as its compromises are set within the context of confession. A helpful reminder, even then, is that confession does not compensate for any treatment of baptism which forfeits the integrity of its symbolic power.

5 Clue

When the compromise of an original position is admitted, the hope of recovering its original purity is much better assured. Baptism's relationship to every segment of the Church's life has been noted. Knowledge of where baptism has been compromised and misused will provide a source of information about a number of the Church's current problems. No real difficulty in the Church has left baptism unaffected. For the same reason, no perplexity is likely to be resolved apart from baptism. It offers a clear view to the center of the Church's defects. If one wishes to diagnose the maladies besetting an ecclesiastical institution, he would do well to take the temperature of the baptismal waters. If he would analyze its neuroses, he may find helpful symptoms in the manner of its administration.

Morrison, who wrote so grudgingly about baptism, was forced to admit, however reluctantly, the centrality of the initiation rite in the modern dilemma of the Church. He inadvertently paid baptism a compliment of considerable proportions. "I am unable," he complained, "to accept the nonchalant counsel of many educated leaders who have themselves been emancipated from the dogma and who say, 'Leave the baptism question alone, get the churches interested

[28] A. Gilmore (ed.), *Christian Baptism* (London: Lutterworth Press, 1959), chap. 8, "The Theology of Baptism," by Neville Clarke, p. 320.

and engaged in the larger human enterprises of religion and the baptism question will solve itself.'

"I do not think it will solve itself.

"And meantime the dogmatic convictions with reference to it stand in the way of our getting those churches to engage themselves wholeheartedly in the more vital interests of religion. . . . It is not because I am so much interested in the baptism question, but because I am profoundly interested in the life and death problem of modern religion that I have let myself be persuaded to write this book and to send it forth." [29]

Morrison was an unwitting prophet in this respect no matter how much he wanted to be otherwise. By his own admission he wrote on baptism because he wanted to get it out of the way. Then he could begin, he felt, to deal with the "life and death" problem of modern religion. But he expressed an inadvertent prophecy in confessing that baptism had to be dealt with, one way or the other, before the intrinsic difficulty and problem of the Church could be confronted. His blind spot is similar to that of other Christians. Many churchmen still do not wish to be bothered with baptism. Along with Morrison they feel that they are forced, in dealing with it, to an unfortunate postponement of their coming to grips with vital issues of the Church. Morrison, and those in agreement with him, are wrong in their judgment that baptism is a dead and irrelevant concern. It is the door to the Church and is thereby the primary clue to the life and death issues with which the Church is involved.

George Every testifies to the clue-like quality of baptism from another perspective. He claims that it is pertinent because it is marked with an ethical dimension. "The Church could," he points out,

and did in the end provide rites for many nations, rituals of initiation to unite Christians with Christ and introduce them to their social and civic responsibilities. No doubt there were and are disadvantages in this connection between baptism and registration, confirmation and training for adult life, but the very fact that this

[29] Charles Clayton Morrison, *The Meaning of Baptism* (Chicago: Disciples Publication Society, 1914), pp. 6-7.

identification could happen does tell us something of the reasons why the Christian Church conquered the mystery religions in the end of the pagan world. These religions were private mysteries divorced from social ethics, incapable of conflict with politics and science. If they changed the self, they changed it back into the free flow of fantasy, bringing release from all sense of responsibility, and escape for the time being into an easier world. But Christians took their converts to the cross, and if they did not always carry it, at least they came back better prepared to bear another's burdens.[30]

Of real moment to our premise is Every's insistence that Christian baptism, the rite of initiation into Christ and His Church, is an ethical act. It does not introduce the convert to a private and more accommodating world but into a demanding community in which he must live as a disciple. Christianity takes its converts to the cross by baptizing them into the death of Jesus Christ. And therein they die to sin. But do they? The Church no longer competes with mystery religions as it had to do in earlier years. There are few modern religions offering escape to an easier world. Contemporary religions, whether Christian or not, are ethically oriented and ethically minded. Those ethics may not be the same as Christian ethics. But these religions do involve their devotees with politics and science. They relate to the world and its welfare. Every's insistence on the ethical note in baptism is consequently all the more important. The Church has little reason to be proud of its commitment to the Christian ethic at present. Since it is no longer competing with the mystery religions, in which the ethical strain was not significant, it cannot point to its own ethical sensitivity as distinctive. Furthermore, it is evident on many sides that other ideologies, many of them of a secular cast, outstrip the Church in some phases of ethical achievement. Athletic teams are racially integrated more easily than churches; Southern academic institutions—private and church-related—have

[30] George Every, *The Baptismal Sacrifice* (London: S.C.M. Press, 1959), pp. 24-25.

probably been integrated because of their need for research grants rather than because of sermons preached in the college chapel; integrated swimming pools in the South are as remote a possibility as can be imagined, but they are likely to come to pass sooner than integrated baptismal pools. The moral discipline of churchmen, in sum, is no longer sufficiently distinctive as to compel the judgment that being a Christian necessarily assures a more moral person.

The recovery of an ethical dimension in the Christian faith is not dependent upon revitalizing the rite of baptism. It is logical, however, to believe that baptism, rightly interpreted and administered, would introduce the convert to the truth that he has been baptized into an ethical community. If and when the baptizing Church takes its converts to the cross, there can be no question about the ethical nature of the faith which they have undertaken.

Baptism serves as clue by virtue of its symbolic quality. The word "symbolic" is used arbitrarily. A discussion of its merits in comparison with "sacrament" or "ordinance" is still to come (cf. pp. 169-174). For the time being, symbol is the representative word and a synonym for any others the reader prefers. Of immediate importance is the realization that because baptism is a symbol, it provides the Church with both conscience and clue which no substitute promises to provide.

This is made plain by P. T. Forsyth, a noted English preacher at the turn of the century. "It is the Church's duty, in our belief," he wrote,

> to see that its ministers deal truly and faithfully with God's Word of Grace. And that is a word which is as real in the sacraments as in the sermons. And, so far as the Church is concerned, it is, in a way, more in the sacraments than in the sermons, because the audible preaching is largely the minister's act, especially in its form, and it reflects his idiosyncrasy (which may dim the truth as well as wing it); but the Sacrament, the declaring of the Word in that visible shape, is chiefly the venerable and unchanging act of the Church, in a form mainly prescribed, massive and historic.

It is the "utterance of the community to which the minister does but lend his voice." [31]

Forsyth established himself as a preacher of ability and dedication. He could hardly be accused of failing to take preaching seriously. He sounds very much like Martin Luther (no inept man in the pulpit), who called baptism "God's word in water." These maxims are not easily dismissed. We are more likely to come to grips with the Church's certainties by a scrutiny of its symbols than by a perusal of its preaching.

An examination of current practices indicates that this opinion is not widely accepted. In many churches, even those of liturgical traditions, the pulpit is the focal point of orthodoxy and spiritual certainty. If the pulpit proclaims that tithing is "God's plan for financing the program," it is assumed that the congregation believes in tithing. This judgment is not affected in the least by the fact that the congregation may not practice tithing to any noticeable degree. Evangelistic preaching is interpreted as an unmistakable sign that a given church is "warmed by the fires of evangelism." The interest a church has in Christian education is often measured by its response to the preacher's plea to reach the goal in Sunday school on a "great rally day." Many churches, North and South, have by now convinced themselves that they are racially inclusive because they permit their preachers, within reasonable limits, of course, to preach openly about the matter. Baptism is the victim of the same general pattern. If the pulpit declares for the sole authenticity of believers' baptism, the act itself makes little difference one way or another.

No wonder Forsyth persists in his support of the "sacraments" as the more trustworthy vehicle of God. Speaking of the rite in particular, he contended: "Baptism is not a small miracle play for didactic effect, but a real act, an act of will; an act of preaching and conveyance on the one side, or worship and confession on the other." [32]

[31] P. T. Forsyth, *Lectures on the Church and Sacraments* (London: Longmans, Green & Co., Ltd., 1917), p. 172.
[32] *Ibid.*, pp. 181-182.

The failure of words confronts us. It lies behind much of what has already been said. Churches, boasting of the absence of the symbolic in their lives, may be guilty of greater arrogance than those adorned with pretentious ecclesiastical trappings. The members of the former type march into an "auditorium" which is conspicuous by its lack of any religious suggestion. There may be flowers, in a vase dripping water and mud on the communion table, connoting the vigor of a fragrant pantheism. The sign of the "old rugged cross" has given way to an "old rugged gladiola." In many such instances, the worshipers wait with an air more of resignation than expectancy for the pulpit to fill the void with words. The minister does not disappoint them. A torrent of words spills out in a variety of tone and rhythm. Reverence requires the sound of a bass voice and a slow pace. The voice of the prophet breaks on the high notes of condemnation. The money-raiser is plaintive. "Peace of mind" is accomplished by a pleasant smile and a businesslike voice. The man who gets things done in his religious huckstering sounds like a radio announcer advertising a product.

Many who realize the truth of the above are not willing to revert to symbol. Instead they go to the extreme of the Quaker. He is no better off; his informal meeting place exhibits the same barrenness. Having discovered the futility of words, many of his number engage in equally futile silence. Can silence say anything? God was a "still, small voice"—not a divine muteness. Does the Holy Spirit come so stealthily? Is He like a thief in the night? Must man hold tongue and breath so as to hear the Spirit's rustle and catch Him before He speeds away? It makes no better sense to fill the silence with silence than to fill the silence with words.

If baptism is to mean again what it should mean to the churches, they must first confess the failure of words. They need not treat this as a tragedy. Out of this failure the symbols of the Church are born and sustained in God's good providence. "It has been pointed out," we are reminded by George Hendry, "that if we could formulate a doctrine of the sacraments that was entirely satisfying, we could then dispense with the sacraments themselves; for the sacraments are the acts that begin at the point where words fail; they are the acts in which the original saving acts of Christ 'reverberate' in their own key and they cannot be transposed into the key of systematic doctrine." [33]

When the mighty acts of God, formed and given in redemptive love, awaken faith in some of us, we are moved to the agony of Simon Peter. We pray for the Lord to leave us because our sense of sin is so acute. This may be, to a degree, because our tongues are too clumsy to form the words of faith-response. We cannot frame what we have seen nor tell of our joy. Our shabby and wayward lives cannot hope to put into deeds what we have been unable to put into words. But we can, in the waters of baptism and with bread and cup, see, hear, and respond to the Word of God. He has given us these symbols for just such a purpose. In these moments, we speak not only our word with Him but also with one another. Sacrament or symbol—it matters little by what word we name the event. That something happens—a divine-human engagement—is what really matters.

The discrepancy between the reports of the Oberlin and Edinburgh committees is due to more than random chance. The circumstances giving rise to the difference are informative. The dilemma concerning the importance of baptism may be better answered when we know these circumstances.

The churches of England and the Continent were long ago impaled upon the rude hook of the question mark which is only now beginning to snare their American counterparts. Members of the churches of England and Europe have long been asking: "What is the Church?" Such inquiry is not born in the classroom. Nor is it likely to stem from the religious environment in which the ecclesiastical institution has been a spectacular success. It comes from the milieu during hard times. It is part of that moment of truth when the Church ponders its future, not as to whether it can exist but whether it should. These people have heard the announcement: "God is dead." This announcement has been taken seriously in their world because of events that indicate that it had better be taken seriously.

[33] George Hendry, *The Gospel of the Incarnation* (Philadelphia: The Westminster Press, 1958), p. 167.

In our spiritual gymnasiums for religious activists, the existence of God does not appear to be the most important matter. If the death of God were established, our religious committees could not afford to be left with nothing to do. At best, they might try to find out what happened to the resurrection. At worst, they might create a new "God."

American churches cannot forever maintain this activism. They are also being faced with the question of the Church. Now we must also begin at the beginning with our answers. The beginning is the act of Christian initiation. No one can hope to answer an inquiry concerning the nature and meaning of the Church without dealing with the manner in which it incorporates its members into its life. Who is brought into the Church and how they are brought into the Church must surely influence what the Church is and what its mission is.

It will not be an easy task to bring the churches back to the central question of baptism. A long time has elapsed since it was a dominant note in Christian theology. Schenck calls attention to a periodical, *The Presbyterial Critic,* dated October, 1885, which spoke in alarming tones to that day: "Just in proportion as Infant Baptism falls into disuse, it is a sign that something is wrong. It is an evidence that the Church is proving false to her organic institution and life; is sliding away from her standards; is loosing from her ancient moorings." [34]

As long as the churches deal carelessly with the baptismal form of their separate traditions, the prospect for serious concern with the question of baptism as a whole is not a bright one. The difficulty in coming upon material, after considerable research, that deals with the question of Christian baptism in its entirety rather than with the disputed forms of the rite speaks for itself. Neville Clarke proposed, to the proponents of believers' baptism, what needs to be proposed and accepted by the proponents of all baptismal forms. "With thought and prayer, patience and understanding, Baptists are summoned," he urged, "to bring the treasure of believers' baptism and expose it to the traffic of the ecumenical market place, sure that, if the talent be

[34] Lewis Bevens Schenck, *The Presbyterian Doctrine of Children in the Covenant* (New Haven, Conn.: Yale University Press, 1940), p. 157.

of God, the Lord of the Church will, in due time, receive his own again with usury." [35]

To show that the Church must bring the treasure of Christian baptism, rather than infant or believers', to the ecumenical market place, to the juncture where the Church confronts the world, to the point of an individual's conversion and incorporation into the believing community, and to the myriad situations these matters entail, is the main reason for this book. Before this situation comes to pass, it will be necessary that the two major baptismal traditions be studied with candor. Only after the private distortions of baptism on the part of these two traditions are exposed and admitted, can we hope for a similar Church confession which embraces all communions.

[35] A. Gilmore (ed.), *Christian Baptism* (London: Lutterworth Press, 1959), chap. 8, "The Theology of Baptism," by Neville Clarke, p. 326.

Chapter Two

THE DEVELOPMENT OF
TWO TRADITIONS

Christian baptism is neither believers' baptism nor infant baptism. Each is a distortion of baptism's original intention and practice. The purpose of this book cannot be served until the two positions have been presented in their strongest light; this affords no great difficulty. As has already been suggested, baptism is given the greatest attention when the traditional positions are in debate with each other. This being so, the best scholars should have given their talents to one or the other side of the controversy. Scholarship is equally imposing on either side. The presentation of the two traditions becomes more difficult when the need for objectivity is realized; it is not easy to find objective statements about Christian baptism. Most books on baptism contend for one doctrine and practice against another. It is unlikely that even the present book, which hopes to speak in an equable and modulated tone, will be accepted as objective and fair by all concerned.

Whatever objectivity may have been achieved calls for an expression of gratitude to a number of scholars holding the opposite view to my own. As a friend exclaimed after reading W. F. Flemington's superb book:[1] "He showed me for the first time how a man can believe in infant baptism and be biblical"—so this endeavor has uncov-

[1] W. F. Flemington, *The New Testament Doctrine of Baptism* (London: S.P.C.K. [Society for Promoting Christian Knowledge] Press, 1953).

35

ered well-devised and scholarly approaches to and for the paedobaptist position. The same refinement of thought and perspective
marks the work of scholars committed to believers' baptism. An
honest evaluation of the arguments for both sides will go far in avoiding a biased opinion.

The reader would do well to realize that he has probably been
conditioned by one doctrine more than another. It is safe to say
that he has read little about Christian baptism and much about
infant baptism or believers' baptism. The same openness of mind
characterized by the above comment on Flemington is called for if
the goal of this book is to be secured. It is important that the reader,
from whatever tradition he may have come, realize that the opposing
theological camp is not devoid of scriptural, historical, and doctrinal
support.

1   The Scriptural Basis for Infant Baptism

The New Testament does not debate the doctrine or the form of
baptism in any way. It may be assumed that baptism was not a
matter for controversy until after the New Testament had been written. Those supporting the position of believers' baptism have a quick
and ready answer for the lack of discussion about baptism in the
New Testament. Absence of debate on the question means that
there was but one kind of baptism; namely, believers' baptism. A
formidable array of New Testament scholars do not agree, and insist
that the New Testament strongly suggests that infant baptism is the
preferred form. Because the burden of proof would seem to rest with
this position from the beginning, the scriptural arguments for infant
baptism will be presented first, followed by an exposition of its historical and theological support.

Among those biblical scholars who contend for the validity of infant baptism, none is more resourceful than Joachim Jeremias, Professor of Theology in the University of Göttingen. The first two paragraphs in his book *Infant Baptism in the First Four Centuries* serve
as the exemplar for most arguments for the scriptural authenticity
of infant baptism.

"The New Testament was written in a missionary situation,"

Jeremias explains. "It is therefore not surprising that we should have to note at the outset that all New Testament statements about baptism without exception relate to missionary baptism—i.e., baptism administered when Jews and Gentiles were received into the fellowship."

If we realize this fact, we shall understand why, in the New Testament statements about baptism, the conversion of adults and their baptism stands right in the middle of the picture. For it is they who are joining the Church, while the children, who are, as it were, hidden in the bosom of the family, cannot claim the same degree of attention. This makes the task which engages us more difficult. Yet luckily we are not entirely without material which enables us to infer an answer to the question "Were the children of converts baptized along with their parents?" [2]

Jeremias answers in the affirmative. He makes use of what is known as the "oikos formula" (*oikos,* Greek, "house") in contending for infant baptism in the New Testament. Both W. F. Flemington and Oscar Cullmann, along with others, rely heavily upon this formula for their support of infant baptism. It relates to the baptism of households as they are recorded in the New Testament. A number of texts refer to such baptisms: "I did baptize also the household of Stephanas. . . ." [3] Lydia's invitation to Paul that he should accept her hospitality is described like this: "And when she was baptized, with her household, she besought us, saying, 'If you have judged me to be faithful to the Lord, come to my house and stay.' " [4] There is also the familiar story of the Philippian jailer, who "was baptized at once, with all his family." [5] These illustrations, although not exhaustive, are sufficient to make apparent what is meant by the oikos formula. Drawing upon research in the Old Testament, Jeremias is

[2] Joachim Jeremias, *Infant Baptism in the First Four Centuries,* trans. David Cairns (Philadelphia: The Westminster Press, 1960), p. 19.
[3] I Cor. 1:16a.
[4] Acts 16:15.
[5] Acts 16:33.

sure that the formula, found there as well, not only includes children along with adults, but refers to children, even small children, in a special sense.[6]

Then he proceeds:

When after these observations we turn to the New Testament, we must keep in mind that the New Testament oikos formula is very early. It occurs as early as A.D. 54 in Paul (I Cor. 1:16), and is to be found independently in Luke, and is therefore to be regarded as a pre-Pauline formula. Thus it comes from a time in which the majority of the members of the churches came from the synagogues and from the circle of the "God fearers" loosely attached thereto. If we grasp this, we shall have to agree . . . that the New Testament oikos formula was adopted from the Old Testament cultic language (and in particular, we may say, from the terminology of circumcision) and introduced into the formal language employed in the primitive Christian rite of baptism; it has the same form and the same meaning as the old biblical ritual formula, i.e., it includes small children as well as others. This does not mean to say that in every particular case in which the baptism of a "whole household" is mentioned, small children were actually present. But it does mean that Paul and Luke could under no circumstances have applied the oikos formula, if they had wished to say that only adults had been baptized.[7]

Jeremias protects himself at this point by refusing to insist that the mention of a whole household incontrovertibly proves that infants were baptized in New Testament times. On the other hand, he suggests that Luke and Paul were not contending for the baptism of believers only when they used the word "household" in the absence of any stipulation that children were not included. The argument is also undergirded by the great part that family solidarity played in the ancient world.

[6] Jeremias, op. cit., p. 20.
[7] Ibid., pp. 21-22.

An inference for infant baptism is skillfully drawn by the same author from a connection between proselyte baptism, as practiced by the Jews, and early Christian baptism. An imposing collection of materials argues that proselyte baptism was practiced by the Jews in pre-Christian times. Proselyte baptism and primitive Christian baptism possessed similarities in terminology, interpretation, and form. Since proselyte baptism was administered to children, Jeremias concludes that the same practice was maintained in early Christian baptism because of the decided correspondence between the two baptismal acts.[8]

W. F. Flemington is another paedobaptist scholar who points to the strong correspondence between infant baptism and proselyte baptism. "There is no direct evidence in the New Testament for the baptism of infants," he begins.

> Various considerations, however, make it highly probable that some form of infant baptism was known and practiced during the period in which the New Testament books were written. Thus the analogy of Jewish proselyte baptism would give some warrant for the usage. If a proselyte on his entry into Judaism had children, it was customary for them to be circumcised and baptized and admitted as proselytes. The fact that the child could not make promises on his own behalf was not regarded as any hindrance. It was argued that such action on behalf of another was permissible so long as it was obviously for his good. This procedure was followed only in respect of children already born to a proselyte before his adherence to Judaism. Any children born subsequently were circumcised but not baptized.[9]

Flemington alertly provides means to close a loophole in his argument. Since baptism was administered only to Gentiles and their children who were being proselytized and was not administered to

---

[8] *Ibid.,* pp. 24-39.
[9] W. F. Flemington, *The New Testament Doctrine of Baptism* (London: S.P.C.K. Press, 1953), pp. 138-139.

these same Gentiles' children who were born after the parents had
been converted, the connection between proselyte baptism and the
Church's infant baptism may appear to be forced. Flemington is
aware that proselyte baptism for the children of parents outside the
community of faith is not completely analogous to the baptism of
infants belonging to parents within the Christian community. He
counters this objection by the use of a second Jewish analogy relying
heavily upon Paul's statement in Colossians: "In him also you were
circumcised with a circumcision made without hands, by putting off
the body of flesh in the circumcision of Christ; and you were buried
with him in baptism, in which you were also raised with him through
faith in the working of God, who raised him from the dead." [10]

"St. Paul viewed baptism as the Christian counterpart of circumcision," Flemington explains. "The fact that this rite was administered
to infants within the covenant would early encourage Christians to
practice infant baptism. Thus baptism was the sign of entry into the
New Covenant, just as circumcision was of entry into the old." [11]

A twofold analogy appears. In speaking of baptism for the infants
of parents who are not Christian, Flemington describes the analogous
act of proselyte baptism. For infants of parents already Christian,
infant baptism is described as a parallel to circumcision.

Others agree that the connection between proselyte infant baptism
and infant baptism in the Christian community in one instance and
the connection between circumcision and infant baptism in another
is not at all forced. There is no doubt but that both circumcision and
proselyte baptism were performed upon adults and infants as they
were brought from the Gentile world into Judaism. Since these two
rites are closely bound together, if either can be said to find fulfillment or repeal in the act of Christian baptism, the relationship of
Christian baptism to the one would also hold for the other.

Oscar Cullmann lends support to a similar premise. He purposely
presents the doctrine of baptism apart from those New Testament
texts which refer to circumcision. "But," he elaborates, "this is not

[10] Col. 2:11-12.
[11] Flemington, *op. cit.*, p. 138.

to accord to these texts a merely secondary meaning. On the contrary, we shall now show that the doctrine and practice of circumcision, and of proselyte baptism which is closely bound up with it, are presuppositions for the whole complicated question of New Testament baptismal doctrine and its consequent practice." [12]

Colossians 2:11-12 is offered as clear evidence that Christian baptism was first a fulfillment and ultimately a repeal of the Jewish circumcision practice. Proselyte baptism was the first to take the place of circumcision. Gradually, with the intermediation of John's baptism, Christian baptism replaced circumcision. John's contribution to this transition is underscored by his insistence that Jews and Gentiles be treated alike in his call for a baptism unto repentance. John made proselytes out of all people; his baptism was for the remission of their sins and to cleanse them from impurity.[13]

Flemington comes to the same conclusion by a different route. Drawing upon Rabbinic evidence, dated at the end of the second century A.D. but reflective of earlier traditions, he points to the controversy over how soon the baptismal bath might follow circumcision. Doubt gradually grew concerning the necessity of both. There were some who argued that circumcision made a full proselyte without subsequent baptism. Others took the opposite position. Flemington believes that he can discern a movement in history where baptism—since circumcision could not be performed upon females—began to gain the ascendancy in order that a uniform rite could be administered to both men and women.[14]

According to Schenck, John Calvin would not have agreed that circumcision was repealed by baptism. But Calvin did place great store by the similarity of Old and New Testament covenants and their designated seals. He was apparently convinced that the Old Testament covenant was sealed by circumcision and that the New Testament covenant was sealed by baptism. Between the Israelites and

---

[12] Oscar Cullmann, *Baptism in the New Testament* (London: S.C.M. Press, 1950), p. 56.

[13] *Ibid.*, p. 62.

[14] W. F. Flemington, *The New Testament Doctrine of Baptism* (London: S.P.C.K. Press, 1953), pp. 5-6.

Christians, equality in grace was expressed not only in the covenants but also by the significance of the two sealing sacraments.[15]

It remained for Cullmann—in agreement with Jeremias and Flemington about the oikos formula and the connection between proselyte baptism, circumcision, and infant baptism—to supply a scriptural apologetic for the baptism of the children of parents already Christian, while they are still infants. His concern with this rather strange situation arose because of his certainty that while the baptism of infants in this category may be held only by implication, the baptism of adults who were children of Christian parents cannot be supported even by implication. Attention is directed to a verse which is often used as a stronghold for the paedobaptist position:

"If any woman has a husband who is an unbeliever, and he consents to live with her, she should not divorce him. For the unbelieving husband is consecrated through his wife, and the unbelieving wife is consecrated through her husband. Otherwise, your children would be unclean, but as it is they are holy." [16]

Prior to interpreting the passage, Cullmann dismisses any idea that the faith of parents or congregation is a substitute for the infant's lack of faith until he has reached the age where it is a possibility. The infant is not dependent upon a vicarious faith or proxy faith. A believing community is necessary to any and all baptisms. He says:

"If faith were lacking in the congregation assembled for the Baptism, it would not be a congregation; and then the Holy Spirit would be absent. But where the believing congregation is, there the Holy Spirit, operating within it and knowing no limitations, has the power to draw an infant into his sphere, just as in the case of all baptized persons who, according to Paul, are 'by one Spirit . . . baptized into one body' of Christ." [17]

No claim is made that the Corinthians passage proves infant baptism. Since it suggests that the child of a believing parent is born holy, the passage is not conclusive for baptism of any kind. On the

[15] Lewis Bevens Schenck, *The Presbyterian Doctrine of Children in the Covenant* (New Haven, Conn.: Yale University Press, 1940), p. 7.

[16] I Cor. 7:13-14.

[17] Oscar Cullmann, *Baptism in the New Testament* (London: S.C.M. Press, 1950), pp. 42-43.

other hand, Cullmann is unwilling to agree with those who use the text to prove that baptism for the children of Christian parents should not take place at all. Instead he concludes that

> this text may certainly be said to presuppose an idea of collective holiness, even when the Baptism of these children is here regarded as dispensable—collective holiness in the sense of a reception into the Body of Christ which follows not upon a personal decision but upon birth from Christian parents, who have received Baptism. Then again this reception represents a divine act of grace independent of men. Thus, whether Paul here denotes the Baptism of a child as unnecessary or not, it is certain that from the idea of holiness represented here there is a direct line to infant Baptism, but none to a Baptism based on a later decision of those sons and daughters who are born in a Christian home.[18]

Cullmann's reasoning is clear. He refuses to read into Scriptures what is not there. At the same time he is sure that, although the Corinthians text is not a conclusive proof of infant baptism, it definitely implies it. There is, however, not even the slightest implication that adults are baptized who were born of Christian parents. Aware that the greatest number of baptismal candidates, whether infants or believers, come from among those who have been born of Christian parents, he realizes that it is advantageous to his position to give evidence of greater scriptural likelihood for the baptism of the infants of Christian parents than for their baptism after they have reached maturity.

The point is made emphatically:

> While I deliberately express myself with all possible caution concerning the historical question of the practice of an infant Baptism in the New Testament, I should like, on the other hand, with all force to emphasize at the outset that there are in the New Testament decidedly fewer traces, indeed none at all, of the Baptism of adults born of parents already Christian and brought up by

[18] *Ibid.*, p. 44.

them. Chronologically such a case would have been possible about the year 50, if not earlier, that is, certainly within New Testament times. . . . Those who dispute the Biblical character of infant Baptism have therefore to reckon with the fact that adult Baptism for sons and daughters born of Christian parents, which they recommend, is even worse attested by the use of New Testament than infant Baptism (for which certain possible traces are discoverable) and indeed lacks any kind of proof.[19]

This is a telling argument. In answer to the accusation that paedobaptists are forced to argue from silence, it points effectively to an absolute silence waiting for an explanation by the proponents of believers' baptism. Excepting the missionary character of the most primitive New Testament baptism, Cullmann is convinced that there is more scriptural support for the baptism of infants than for adults so far as the progeny of Christian parents is concerned.

Allan Richardson's arguments for the New Testament practice of infant baptism are less cautious than the usual. He agrees that the concept of "solidarity of the family" or the household is not easily dismissed as support for the practice of infant baptism. He objects to Cullmann's tentative proposal that the correct exegesis of I Corinthians 7:14 reads that such children need no baptism since they are holy by reason of their birth. As he sees it, Paul assumes that the children of believing parents have become holy because they have been baptized. A believing parent would inevitably have his child baptized, and this would account for the child's holiness. There is a distinction between the holiness of the children by virtue of their baptism and the sanctification of either the unbaptized husband or wife as a result of being married to a believer. Furthermore, the status of the unbaptized parent, though sanctified, is not equal to that of the baptized child of the believing parent.[20]

Richardson concurs that there is no evidence for the baptism of children of Christian parents when those children have reached adult-

[19] *Ibid.*, p. 26.
[20] Allan Richardson, *An Introduction to the Theology of the New Testament* (New York: Harper & Row, Publishers, 1958), pp. 358-359.

hood. "We may agree with Cullmann," he writes, "when he says that the one thing for which there is no evidence or justification in the NT is the practice of baptizing the children of Christian parents only after they have grown up. If the children are already 'holy' though unbaptized, it is clear that their baptism, since it does not make them 'saints,' is not what is meant by baptism in the NT." [21] Endeavoring to render believers' baptism ineffectual regarding the children of Christian parents, he contends that children become saints through their baptism if they are the children of Christian parents. No meaning or justification for baptism may be found, according to the New Testament, if the children are holy by virtue of their birth. Contenders for believers' baptism cannot logically accept Paul's statement about children being holy by virtue of their birth from a Christian parent. If they do this, they cannot justify baptism of any kind. If, on the other hand, it is argued that children are not holy by virtue of this kind of birth, and if Paul called them holy, then they must have become holy as a result of their baptism when they were infants.

Perhaps the most distinctive aspect of Richardson's argument stems from his comprehensive view of the New Testament:

> Recent NT scholarship has emphasized the organic connection that exists between the worship and practice of the earliest Christian communities and the actual words of the NT records, particularly those of the various pericopae of the Gospels. The records, that is to say, arise out of the inner life and faith of the apostolic Church. In the light of recent NT scholarship there can be no reasonable doubt that the practice of baptizing in infancy the children of Christian parents goes back to the days of the apostles themselves. [22]

It may then be assumed that recorded anecdotes of the life of Christ are representative, to some degree, of the beliefs and practices of the apostolic community. Mark 10:13-16 is a favorite passage of

[21] *Ibid.,* p. 359.
[22] *Ibid.,* p. 358.

this kind, for the paedobaptists, in its implied relationship to the practice of infant baptism.

In receiving the little children, the Church receives Christ himself; the real living Christ is present in the sacrament of holy baptism, for this is where the παιδια (little children) are received into it. The meaning of the passage (Mark 9:36) is made clearer in Mark 10:13-16. Most of the pericopae which St. Mark included in his gospel were selected because they had an important bearing upon some urgent question of faith or discipline in the apostolic Church, and it is likely that this pericope is included because it gives the word of the Lord which the Church understands to represent his mind upon the question of the baptism of infants. Jesus is indignant with those who would prevent the little children from coming to him: 'Suffer the little children to come unto me and forbid them not, for of such is the kingdom of God.' [23]

Two lines of thought support Richardson's conclusion about this pericope. He is sure that it portrays the mind of Christ, as the Church understood it, as an affirmative vote for infant baptism. First of all, Cullmann has collected enough evidence to connect the "forbid them not" with the question "What hinders?" as they belonged to the baptismal rite of the early Church.[24] In the second place, Mark 10:16 is the "literal description of the minister's action at the baptism of infants, then as now. It should be noted that the verse supplies evidence that the laying on of hands was an essential part of the baptismal action of the apostolic Church even when παιδια (little children) were being baptized. St. Mark clearly expected his catechists to use this story as a lesson-illustration when instructing the catechumens upon the meaning of baptism. His intention was well understood by the Church of later centuries, for this passage was read as a baptismal lection for early times." [25]

[23] *Ibid.*, pp. 360-361.

[24] Oscar Cullmann, *Baptism in the New Testament* (London: S.C.M. Press, 1950), pp. 71-80.

[25] Allan Richardson, *An Introduction to the Theology of the New Testament* (New York: Harper & Row, Publishers, 1958), p. 361.

Four major arguments for the scriptural support of the practice of infant baptism have been supplied. The oikos formula, in which the head of the household was the representative for the house, is the first one. It is assumed that mention of the baptism of a household must have included the baptism of infants in some instances at the very least. The second argument draws direct lines between proselyte baptism and circumcision, each of which was administered to infants, and primitive Christian baptism by way of John's rite at the Jordan. A third is Cullmann's contribution concerning the status of children born of Christian parents. They are holy by birth in these circumstances. Richardson counters that they are holy because the believing parent or parents have had them baptized. However, either interpretation attests to the fact that infant baptism is, at least, implied in the New Testament, while children born of believing parents are nowhere explicitly or implicitly baptized when they have become adults. The final conclusion deals with Jesus' reception of little children. Mark 10:13-16 and similar passages, both Cullmann and Richardson contend, are very much like the early baptismal liturgies. Richardson is less cautious than Cullmann in this regard and asserts that the passage in Mark was written by the author as a catechism for infant baptism.

2   The Historical Basis for Infant Baptism

Although the biblical basis for infant baptism is sturdier than might at first be supposed, paedobaptists generally agree that an argument from scripture is not their strongest point. The conviction that history is on their side doubtlessly explains much of their amenability in this respect.

Jeremias writes confidently:

> The statements of Origen, Hippolytus, and Tertullian, which all carry us back into the second century, are of outstanding importance; they constitute the scaffolding which supports the rest of the evidence. . . . Everywhere, with the exception of Eastern Syria, we find in the second century infant baptism as an old and established usage of the Great Church, which both East and West

agree in tracing back to the Apostles. The evidence applies equally to children of Christian and pagan parents. Tertullian alone made a difference between the two groups; his advice to postpone the baptism of children referred to the children of pagan parents and to them alone. Nowhere was there any ground adduced for the baptism of children of Christian parents, not even in Tertullian. On the contrary the East and the West, as far as our information extends, are unanimous in naming the age of infancy (Irenaeus), more precisely the first days after birth (Origen and Cyprian) as the age for baptism. The inscriptions which begin in the West about 200, confirm in detail the picture supplied by the literary sources.[26]

Tertullian's proposal that baptism should be postponed stemmed from his fear of sin's return after the rite had been performed. He believed that defection in the wake of baptism incurred a greater guilt. Having qualified Tertullian's concept as applicable only to the children of pagan parents, infant baptism is presumed to have been the norm by the second century. If by this time it had achieved normality, it must have been noticeably in practice for an appreciable period before.

The martyr Polycarp affords an interesting and significant study with respect to the baptism of infants. Jeremias believes that his death occurred in the period 167-168 A.D.[27] The reader is advised to read more extensively in the matter if he is not satisfied with this date of Polycarp's martyrdom. Since Jeremias' argument for the historicity of infant baptism is being studied, the date he sets is arbitrarily accepted for the purpose of his argument. In any event, when Polycarp, the Bishop of Smyrna, was pressured to revile Christ, he answered: "For eighty-six years I have served him, and he never did me any wrong. How can I blaspheme my King who saved me?" [28] The conjecture that Polycarp may have been speaking of a baptism in his adolescent years is illogical. This would mean that he was a

[26] Joachim Jeremias, *Infant Baptism in the First Four Centuries,* trans. David Cairns (Philadelphia: The Westminster Press, 1960), p. 86.

[27] *Ibid.,* p. 62.

[28] *Ibid.,* p. 60.

hundred years old at his martyrdom. In itself this is not inconceivable. It would also mean that he had traveled from Smyrna to Rome when he was ninety years old or more. This borders on the impossible. Therefore, if Polycarp was put to death near the age of eighty-six, this would place his baptism close to the year 81 or 82 A.D. From this material, Jeremias draws two conclusions. Polycarp was baptized as an infant. The age of eighty-six at the time of his death means that this baptism took place near the end of the first century.

Indirect arguments for the early beginning of infant baptism are plentiful. The opponents of this position quite naturally draw different inferences from similar material. A. W. Argyle, for example, not only disagrees with the date of Polycarp's death but also interprets his statement in a different way. The date of martyrdom is set at 155 A.D. If this date were accepted and Polycarp had been baptized as an infant, the time of that baptism would be near the year 70 A.D. Argyle's dates force him to propose an earlier date for infant baptism than most supporters of the rite are willing to accept. The enjoinder against infant baptism, in view of his own date for the death of the Bishop, is somewhat lame. He reasons that Polycarp may have been serving the Lord before he was baptized. Whether this strikes a death blow at the possibility of Polycarp's baptism as an infant is a moot question. What is more important is that a theological note has been sounded which cannot possibly belong to the main stream of baptismal doctrine of any form.[29]

A great amount of time and argument has been spent on determining just when infant baptism began and when it became the norm. As has already been seen, Jeremias believes it was practiced during the first century, even during apostolic times, and that it had become a normal procedure by the end of the second century. There are many historians and scholars who stoutly contest this early date. On the other hand, Argyle, in the source just quoted, does concede that by the fifth century infant baptism had become the more general if not almost the regular practice of the Church. Little value to the aim of our endeavor lies in pursuing the exact time at which

[29] A. Gilmore (ed.), *Christian Baptism* (London: Lutterworth Press, 1959), chap. 5, "Baptism in the Early Centuries," by A. W. Argyle, p. 197.

infant baptism began and in which it was adopted as the prevailing practice. All agree that for at least fifteen of the twenty centuries of the history of the Church, infant baptism not only has been practiced but has been predominant in the Christian Church. This is an overwhelming fact of history and one in which the paedobaptists take great confidence.

The great conflict between infant baptism and believers' baptism so colors the written history of the rite that a history of Christian baptism is not easily come by. It may be that no other kind of baptismal history is possible. Whatever the cause, each tradition is comfortably ensconced in its own preferred history. The suspicion grows that each has its reasons for having become so. When these reasons are uncovered, the absence of a general history of baptism will be more easily understood, although not justified.

P. T. Forsyth presents a plea reflecting an admission to this continuing and unmediated bias. "It would be well," he counseled, "to accept the historic situation by at least making the question an open one in the same church, with either practice at choice. . . . Would Christianity really be reformed by abolishing infant Baptism? Can that now be hoped for? Is that the only way to keep magic out? Would it not be burning the house to roast the pig? Would it not reduce the Church to the permanent condition of a missionary Church only, amid a quite pagan society?" [30]

The attempt to palliate the conflict by this kind of compromise has not met with success. The implacability of both sides is not the chief reason that Forsyth's plea has gone unheeded. Whether it is a conscious or unconscious motive, each side of the debate seems aware that so long as the argument continues unabated the misuse of baptism by all segments of the Church will hardly be noticed.

3   The Theological Argument for Infant Baptism

The changed status of the Church from that of its New Testament mission is immensely important to the paedobaptist polemic. It willingly admits that the Church was initially in a missionary situation.

---

[30] P. T. Forsyth, *Lectures on the Church and Sacraments* (London: Longmans, Green & Co., Ltd., 1917), p. 168.

This means that the converts were brought from the pagan camp or from the legalism of Judaism. A new religion cannot deal with children. It must deal with adults. It recruits those who embrace it with maturity, give impetus to its doctrine, and commit themselves to its ethic. The missionary nature of the Church was compounded by the expectation of the imminent return of Christ to claim His victory over sin and death. The prospect of an established Church did not impress itself upon the New Testament writers. Since they did not think of the institution in these terms, they did not think of baptism in these terms. When the Church did become a more permanent community of faith with the promise of tenure in the world, its theology was affected. One of the first questions plaguing adult Christians was the status of their children in terms of salvation and church membership. They logically assumed a difference between their children, who were born in Christian homes, and converts, who came out of pagan or other environments. Christian parents recognized that their children were born in a setting distinct from that of their own birth. Occupied with its own establishment and with its children, the Church found a solution to these multiple problems through the faith and practice of infant baptism.

One of the strongest opponents of infant baptism among contemporary voices is R. E. O. White of England. At the same time, he has not underestimated the power and legitimate appeal of the doctrine. He has listed what he considers to be the four strongest theological values within the paedobaptist stronghold. They are (a) the prevenience of divine grace, (b) a better harmony with the biblical doctrine of the covenant, (c) a more objective view of corporate salvation, and (d) a safeguard for the notion of a true sacrament.[31]

This makes for a fair and accurate tribute to the theological persuasion of infant baptism. Those who belong to the tradition which White opposes can do their doctrine no greater justice, in this sense, than has this English Baptist.

Allan Richardson makes capital of the first point in his emphasis upon the antecedent love of God with respect to baptism. He be-

[31] R. E. O. White, *The Biblical Doctrine of Initiation* (Grand Rapids, Mich.: Wm. B. Eerdmans Publishing Co., 1960), chap. 16.

lieves that the death of Christ, as the baptism of the human race, was not the result of man's faith but the cause of it. The same is true for the baptism of the individual. Baptism theologically precedes the awakening of man's faith rather than being consequent to it. "Baptism," he continues, "is the sacrament and effective symbol of justification and, especially at the baptism of infants, it powerfully proclaims the antecedent love of God by whose prevenient grace all the virtues, including that of faith, are imparted through the gift of the Holy Spirit."[32]

Paedobaptists agree that this strikes a decisive blow for infant baptism. Whatever the efforts to the contrary, believers' baptism, according to its detractors, cannot escape the danger of emphasizing the act of the believer rather than that of God's grace. The baptism of a helpless and unknowing infant accents the grace of God as the initiator and sustainer of redemption. [The moment human response to an act of God is highlighted, the difficulty lies with keeping that response from evolving into the stature of an initial cause.]Paedobaptists rightfully contend that no such problem attends the act of infant baptism.

John Calvin's theology of adoption and the biblical doctrine of the covenant were immediately in accord. The relationship between infant baptism and the biblical doctrine of the covenant is thereby strengthened. Calvin was quick to shield his doctrine from the accusation of magic by a notable distinction. Baptism had a twofold grace as he understood it. It offered remission of sins and the regeneration of life. Since it would have been exceedingly difficult to provide evidence of regeneration in the conduct of an infant, he distinguished between remission or sin and regeneration by assigning a different time schedule for each. Remission of sin was instantaneous and complete at the moment of baptism. Regeneration proceeded gradually. It was as if the infant were given a regenerative capsule at baptism filled with tiny pellets which dissolved and gave off their spiritual therapy at different stages in his life.

Against this background, Calvin proceeded to link infant baptism

---

[32] Allan Richardson, *An Introduction to the Theology of the New Testament* (New York: Harper & Row, Publishers, 1958), p. 363.

with covenantal adoption: "The offspring of believers are born holy, because their children, while yet in the womb, before they breathe the vital air, have been adopted into the covenant of eternal life. Nor are they brought into the Church by Baptism on any other ground than because they belonged to the body of the Church before they were born. . . . Baptism must, therefore, be preceded by the gift of adoption, which is not the cause of a half salvation merely, but gives salvation entire; and this salvation is afterwards ratified by baptism." [33]

God's love and His loyalty to the covenant relationship with His people are never absent from Calvinism. No one can inveigh successfully against its baptismal theology if he leaves his doctrine of either or both election and adoption intact. The theory of a progressive regeneration guards against the stigma of magic. Calvin confuses the proponents of believers' baptism by agreeing with them that baptism is a ratifying act—both a sign and a seal. This is precisely what so many of his opponents insist upon calling it. He disagrees with them, however, in his insistence that baptism comes to pass by God's act of election and is in no wise dependent upon man's belief or an act of trust.

J. S. Whale enhances White's third admission with lancet-like logic. He pinpoints infant baptism's indispensable contribution to the "objective giveness" of the Gospel of Redemption. In this manner the significance of infant baptism is threefold: "First, it guards against the menace of mere subjectivism. . . . In the second place, infant baptism guards against the irrelevant fancy known as 'dedicatory baptism,' whereby parents who know no better suppose that in this rite they are dedicating the child to God. . . . In the third place, the practice and doctrine of infant baptism has been and is the great historical guarantee of the Church as something more than loose local associations of believers." [34]

The sacrament of infant baptism is a garment finely spun as Whale

[33] John Calvin, *Tracts and Treatises* (Grand Rapids, Mich.: Wm. B. Eerdmans Publishing Co., 1958), III, "In Defense of the Reformed Faith," p. 85.

[34] J. S. Whale, *Christian Doctrine* (London and Glasgow: Fontana Books, 1957), pp. 158-159.

weaves it through and through with objectivity as the thread of his argument. Redemption is needed at that very juncture of life where a subjective response is not possible. Such is the status of an infant. Whale's consistent concern with objective salvation comes to focus in his attack upon the act of "dedicatory baptism." He relentlessly reduces this to frivolous sentimentality. Without saying as much, he recognizes that there is just as much subjectivity in the act of parents dedicating their children to God as could possibly be in believers' baptism. What Christ has already done on the cross for the child is the main fact of infant baptism. This should never be obscured by the "sweet service" of dedication. Baptism is not an act of faith by a believer or a parent but by the Church.

If White were looking for an advocate of his fourth point, he could find none better than Donald Baille, who concurs that infant baptism safeguards the notion of the true sacrament. Baille poses an astute question:

> . . . if baptism is a sacrament, a means of grace, in which the recipient receives in faith the benefits of the Gospel, and thus has his faith strengthened, then the question inevitably rises whether this can in any sense be true of an infant who is incapable of exercising faith and who is unconscious of the whole proceeding.[35]

Before giving his answer, Baille asserts that the benefits of the gospel are to be received in faith. He also avoids the guilt of sacramental magic, as the note of faith never wavers throughout his statements on baptism.

> I would begin my answer by pointing out that the sacrament of baptism brings the child into a new environment, the environment of the Church of Christ, which Calvin, following Cyprian, called the Mother of all who have God as their Father . . . a baby must have the grace of God in order that it may grow as a

[35] D. M. Baille, *The Theology of the Sacraments* (New York: Charles Scribner's Sons, 1947), p. 82.

truly Christian child. And it is through the faith and love of the Church and the parents, directed upon the child through physical channels and using the effective symbolism of baptism that the grace of God reaches the scarcely conscious child.[36]

Accordingly, baptism ushers the child into an environment of grace. No child can grow up as a Christian without it. This is accomplished through the sacramental act of baptism in which the child is incorporated into the Church. Baille combines the faith and love of both parents and the Church as twin necessities by which the grace of God ultimately reaches the child.

There are other salient points proclaiming the theological value of infant baptism. They are not necessary to our purpose. Each of the foregoing principles is strong and vigorous in its own right. Furthermore, these are truths which, as we have seen in White's position, are visible to the watchful eyes of those who are anything but friendly to the practice of infant baptism. Most certainly, then, these powerful doctrinal pillars are not unknown to the proponents of the paedobaptist faith. They have been developed. They are not unprotected from attack by the opposite camp. Also, they are quite formidable truths, which might possibly completely undermine the position of those who uphold the practice of believers' baptism.

His inconsistency notwithstanding, Martin Luther was a formidable protagonist for paedobaptist doctrines. Whenever he spoke on the problem of baptism, his was a voice lending rugged strength to the doctrine of infant baptism. A summary of the theological arguments for this position can do no better than to look to the Reformer.

Having jettisoned the doctrine of baptism of any aspect which might gain the approval of the Anabaptists, he spoke with evident and unrestrained fury. "Thus the devil would secretly teach us to build upon our works," he warned,

and in order to accomplish this more easily he makes a sham of faith and says: "If you do not believe you are not baptized." But it simply does not follow that, if I do not obey my parents, there-

[36] *Ibid.*

fore I have no parents; if I do not obey the government, therefore, the government is nothing. So it does not follow here; that a person has not received baptism in faith, therefore, the baptism is nothing or is not genuine. Indeed, the baptism was genuine precisely because you did not rightly receive it. The abuse confirms the baptism but does not deny it. If all of you here were to be baptized today and there were hardly three among you who were holy, the baptism would still not be false, but rather the contrary; for our work and misuse neither make nor unmake God's work.[37]

Luther spoke to the contrary many times in his comments on baptism. What he said in the above passage is of consequence, nevertheless. To his credit, whenever he whittled the doctrine of baptism down to the bare bone of his faith, God's work was always paramount. He saw and understood infant baptism as the work of God.

4 · The Scriptural Basis for Believers' Baptism

The same general procedure may be followed in developing the argument for believers' baptism as was done for the baptism of infants. This is to take notice of the scriptural, historical, and theological categories.

The scriptures give confidence to the exponents of believers' baptism. As was done with White's admission concerning the theology of infant baptism, it is possible to use the opposition's statements to prove the point.

More than once in our study of the New Testament evidence attention has been called to the fact that in the New Testament times the typical Christian baptism was that of an adult believer. As we saw in the Acts, baptism was the regular response of those who "heard" or "received the word," who "repented and be-

[37] Martin Luther, *Luther's Works,* trans. John W. Doberstein (Philadelphia: Muhlenberg Press, 1959), LI, 186.

lieved." . . . New Testament statements about baptism cannot all be used in reference to infant baptism without modification. We must frankly recognize that much harm has been done, and a superstitious attitude to baptism too often encouraged, because New Testament language, used originally of believers' baptism, has been applied indiscriminately as it stands, to the baptism of infants.[38]

These are the words of an able New Testament scholar who persuasively promotes the cause of infant baptism. We have had the words of Jeremias in the same vein. He concurs that the New Testament material describes believers' baptism almost without exception. The concept of hearing and receiving the word, of repenting and believing, in connection with baptism is a happy introduction to New Testament teaching about the rite. Only baptisms of faith receive mention in the New Testament.

"The discussion about baptism," writes Johannes Schneider in consequence, "resolves itself in the end into the question: Which baptism is scriptural, infant baptism or believers' baptism? A baptism which requires faith and a personal confession of faith, or baptism which admits no faith on the part of the candidate and postpones confession of faith until a later time? All confessions agree that baptism is not an end in itself. Those who require it as a sacrament do not completely separate it from faith. The real issue is what is the place of baptism in the scheme of salvation." [39]

Schneider will not settle for a baptism in which faith is not present in the act. His immediate reduction of the question of baptism concerning its place in salvation is important to the over-all scheme. By asking such a question, he distinguishes himself from all who insist that baptism is no more than an "outward and visible sign of an inward and invisible act." He uses the term "effective bap-

[38] W. F. Flemington, *The New Testament Doctrine of Baptism* (London: S.P.C.K. Press, 1953), pp. 134-135.

[39] Johannes Schneider, *Baptism and Church in the New Testament* (London: Carey Kingsgate Press, Ltd., 1957), p. 7.

tism" to describe what he considers to be its central importance, meaning that something is accomplished in the act and that it is more than a mere token.

Galatians provides material in which the idea of effective baptism takes form. ". . . in Christ Jesus you are all sons of God, through faith. For as many of you as were baptized into Christ have put on Christ." [40] The key words in this verse are faith and baptism. To be "sons of God, through faith" is also correlative with "putting on Christ." Consequently, one does not put on Christ by being baptized into Christ without an act of faith. That would make baptism an act of magic. Faith and baptism are reciprocal. A mystery is involved in our putting on Christ through baptism. Faith is the necessary ingredient of that mystery. Baptism is "effective baptism" because it uses man's faith to baptize him into Christ. The implication is unavoidable that faith alone, without baptism, would not enable the man to put on Christ.

Paul's experience with the Philippian jailer may be interpreted in a similar vein. Acts records the jailer's consternation at the miracle of opening doors and falling fetters before the onslaught of the hymns and prayers of Paul and Silas. Convicted of sin, the jailer crys out: ". . . 'Men, what must I do to be saved?' And they said, 'Believe in the Lord Jesus, and you will be saved, you and your household.' And they spoke the word of the Lord to him and to all that were in his house. And he took them the same hour of the night, and washed their wounds, and he was baptized at once, with all his family." [41]

Schneider does not hesitate to deal differently with the oikos formula than the paedobaptists do. Paul's first word to his warden was that he should believe in Jesus Christ. Faith is called for prior to baptism. Also, the word of the Lord was proclaimed to all who were in that house. Proclaiming the word of the Lord to an infant calls for imagination, to say the least. Faith is not to be separated from salvation or any act thereof.[42]

---

[40] Gal. 3:26-27.
[41] Acts 16:30-33.
[42] Schneider, *op. cit.*, p. 39.

In the book of Acts, wherever baptism is mentioned, the hearing and receiving of the word is its justification. The necessity of faith does not alone make the case for believers' baptism. Flemington and Cullmann have already confirmed the relationship between faith and baptism. Others who have not made it their emphasis would not deny its place in baptism. The locus of faith is the central question. Some paedobaptists, appealing to the solidarity of the family in Judaism, contend for the sufficiency of parental faith. Others insist upon the believing church or congregation. Still others declare that parental and congregational faith are mutually necessary. Cullmann's sage comment that this faith is not a proxy for an infant is worthy of recall. Actually, he locates necessary faith in the congregation for any and all kinds of baptism. Believers' baptism cannot establish its argument by an appeal to the presence of faith alone at baptism. It must prove that such faith is necessarily the possession of the one being baptized.

White does not run from this demand for faith's particularity if believers' baptism is to be taken seriously. He attacks the twin supports of the paedobaptist position; namely, the concept of family solidarity and that of religious corporateness. Jeremiah's pronouncement of the "new covenant" marks the time when the "centre of gravity in religious experience is shifted from the nation to the individual, and membership is not a racial but a moral and spiritual matter." [43] The prophet's words are not taken as support for religious experience that is purely private and individualistic. They do propose that the basis for religious corporateness no longer be determined by genealogy. Parenthetically, Paul's explanation in the letter to Rome appears to support this premise: "For not all who are descended from Israel belong to Israel, and not all are children of Abraham because they are his descendants; but 'Through Isaac shall your descendants be named.' This means that it is not the children of the flesh who are the children of God, but the children of the promise are reckoned as descendants." [44]

[43] R. E. O. White, *The Biblical Doctrine of Initiation* (Grand Rapids, Mich.: Wm. B. Eerdmans Publishing Co., 1960), p. 31.
[44] Rom. 9:6b-8.

Referring to the remnant in Isaiah's prophecy, White contends that it should be understood in this same light. The remnant's qualification for its existence was not dependent upon racial or historical origins. It was constituted on the basis of its faith-response to the deliverance of God upon His own initiative. White concludes that "others, possessing all the historical, hereditary, and 'accidental' credentials of the chosen people, but lacking the qualifications of faith, character and spiritual experience, are henceforth excluded from the covenant, and from participation in the forward-moving purposes of God which the covenant-people serve." [45]

In judging the effectiveness of White's argument one must note that it does not apply as widely as might be first supposed. It does cause some discomfort to hold to the concept of parental faith as proxy for the faith of the infant. It fails to come to grips with the religious corporateness in which the baptism of the infant takes place within and as a result of the believing congregation. The fact that such a congregation is gathered on moral and spiritual grounds rather than by racial dimension does not affect the general idea of corporateness.

Although this argument successfully disposes of a covenant community determined by racial or genealogical considerations, it falls short of ascertaining the locus of the faith necessary to Christian baptism. Disposing of the efficacy of faith by virtue of parental proxy answers no more than a part of the question. It does not controvert the main emphasis of Cullmann, who claims that faith residing in a believing congregation is necessary to any baptism. This faith, in itself, is not sufficient. Contrary to Cullmann's opinion, the one being baptized must also possess faith. The attempt to make faith categorical in this instance has been disastrous for the supporters of believers' baptism. Their position is sounder when faith is inimical to the act of baptism on the part of everyone involved. It is not wise to attempt to make congregational faith of no account in order to counteract the claim that the faith of the one baptized is irrelevant. Actually the faith of the one baptized can no

[45] White, *op. cit.*, p. 39.

more substitute for a faithless congregation than can the believing congregation substitute for a faithless candidate for baptism.

Another major meaning of baptism found throughout the New Testament is that of identification with Christ in His death, burial, and resurrection. In this instance the reciprocal power of the baptism of Jesus by John and the baptism of those who would be the followers of Jesus has not been sufficiently developed. In short, one cannot understand the New Testament meaning of baptism into Christ unless he has some sense of the New Testament meaning of Christ's baptism by John's hand.

It is impossible to rid the Johannine baptism of its clear connotation of repentance, cleansing, and the remission of sins. This element of the Jordan rite is unmistakable. The gospel makes it clear, however, that Jesus did not undergo baptism on these terms: "Then Jesus came from Galilee to the Jordan to John, to be baptized by him. John would have prevented him, saying, 'I need to be baptized by you, and do you come to me?' " [46]

If the baptism of Jesus was neither for the purpose of cleansing and remission, nor an act of repentance, we are still in a quandary as to its central purpose. The gospel of Matthew attempts an answer. Setting and context are important. Baptism, by John's hand, was offered not only to pagan but also to Jew. Sin had infested the whole of mankind. All were in need of cleansing. John's baptism was more than the proselyte baptism practiced by the Jews. They, as well as Gentiles, were invited to plunge into the searchingly uncomfortable waters of baptism in the Jordan: "But when he saw many of the Pharisees and Sadducees coming for baptism, he said to them, 'You brood of vipers! Who warned you to flee from the wrath to come? Bear fruit that befits repentance and do not presume to say to yourselves, "We have Abraham as our father"; for I tell you, God is able from these stones to raise up children to Abraham. Even now the axe is laid to the root of the trees; every tree therefore that does not bear good fruit is cut down and thrown into the fire.' " [47]

[46] Matt. 3:13-14.
[47] Matt. 3:7-10.

Jesus availed Himself of the Johannine baptism which sought to embrace the whole of humanity. Since His righteousness rules out the need for cleansing and repentance, His baptism must be understood "against the background of the announcement just made concerning the Messianic judge of the world and his baptism. Only thus can the question of John and Jesus' answer be understood. The time of my baptism is over, now comes the time of your baptism with the Spirit and with Fire. What then does the following mean? The Messianic baptiser is one to be baptised, the judge of the world is among the sinners." [48]

Baptism at the hands of John was the act by which Christ identified Himself with sinful and suffering humanity. He identified not only as "judge among sinners" but as Saviour among the suffering. Other meanings may be adduced from the baptism of Jesus. There are elements of renunciation and dedication in His baptism. Christ's acceptance of His particular mission in the world is not to be ignored. These do not detract from the central fact of His identification with humankind. Man, refusing to be like God, had left his broken image behind in the dust of a spoiled and barren Eden when he was expelled from the garden. Now, in the ministry of reconciliation, God became like man in Jesus of Nazareth. It was clear that this identification with man made Christ no less the Son of God. For at His baptism, God spoke with the pride of a Father: "This is my beloved Son, with whom I am well pleased." [49]

Identification with humanity through baptism was given its ultimate interpretation by Jesus Himself. Baptism and His death were inseparable. And this death was death on the cross. There was the judgment to which Bornkamm has alluded in His baptism. Luke's account reads, " 'I came to cast fire upon the earth; and would that it were already kindled! I have a baptism to be baptized with; and how I am constrained until it is accomplished!' " [50] It is generally agreed that this is the word of Christ Himself. It can have no other meaning than a connection between baptism and death. The same

[48] Gunther Bornkamm, *Jesus of Nazareth* (New York: Harper & Row, Publishers, 1960), p. 48.
[49] Matt. 3:17.
[50] Luke 12:49-50.

is true of the encounter between Christ and the brash sons of Zebedee. The connection here is even more vivid. James and John tried to reserve two of the choicest seats for the great finale of the eschatological drama. They treated Jesus like an enterprising ticket agent. He reacted to this pressure with His searching and daring question, "You do not know what you are asking. Are you able to drink the cup that I drink, or to be baptized with the baptism with which I am baptized?" [51]

Those favoring believers' baptism may draw heavily upon the fact that this is not the kind of question one puts to infants. Jesus declared the symbolic relationship between baptism and death, both for Himself and His followers. A disciple is called through baptism to the cross. In most communions, the cup is not offered the little child even if he has been baptized. He is not able to judge his commitment to Christ nor to the way of the cross. That is reserved for the believer. He is baptized with the fire of the Spirit.

Paul extended the concept of baptismal identification with Christ by adding the joy of the resurrection. Before proceeding in this vein, a brief consideration of Paul's basic attitude toward the rite is appropriate.

Although he makes considerable use of Paul's doctrine of baptism, Emil Brunner is convinced that baptism was not a fundamental concern for the Apostle. He admits that chapter 6 of Romans indicates to the contrary and that here

> Baptism is the point of transition from the death of the old man to the new being and life in Christ. Thus the act of Baptism as such was simply regarded as one with the inner event, so that it might appear that without the act of Baptism the inner event would not have taken place.[52]

Brunner is unwilling to let the matter rest here, and goes on to say:

---

[51] Mark 10:37-38.
[52] Emil Brunner, *Dogmatics*, Vol. III, "The Christian Doctrine of the Church, Faith and the Consummation," trans. David Cairns in collaboration with T. H. L. Parker (Philadelphia: The Westminster Press, 1962), p. 274.

But the whole of the rest of Paul's religious and Christian witness is against this interpretation, as is the fact that he speaks of baptizing with a certain casualness, when he says thank God that he baptized no one in the congregation at Corinth except Crispus and Gaius, and, as it comes to his mind afterwards, also Stephanas and his household. . . . And indeed he says this at the very point where with the greatest precision he avers that he laid the foundation of the same community. The man who speaks thus cannot possibly regard the act of Baptism as something fundamental.[53]

Paul's statement to the Corinthians can mean just the opposite of Brunner's interpretation of it. He was worried about the divisions within the Church. The Apostle was assuredly not casually but deeply concerned about that division. It stretches the imagination to accept his casualness about baptism or anything else under these conditions. Furthermore, Brunner implies that, if Paul were casual about baptism, he was not justified in being so. He writes:

. . . it is clear that purely interior loyalty to Christ must be considered as a loyalty which has not matured to its full reality. The visibility of the Ecclesia is surely one of its essential marks. If we belong to Christ, then we belong to the Ecclesia, just as necessarily as the reality of faith depends on its expressing itself effectually in love.[54]

Chapter 6 of Romans contains much of the core of the Pauline symbolism with respect to baptism: "Do you not know that all of us who have been baptized into Christ Jesus were baptized into his death? We were buried therefore with him by baptism into death, so that as Christ was raised from the dead by the glory of the Father, we too might walk in newness of life. For if we have been united with him in a death like his, we shall certainly be united with him in a resurrection like his." [55]

[53] *Ibid.*, pp. 53-54.
[54] *Ibid.*, pp. 42-43.
[55] Rom. 6:3-5.

This is not a mystical relationship but a plunge into the historic deed of Christ on the cross. Our newness of life is likewise more than a state of mind; it determines the nature of our lives on earth, here and now.

A relationship between Jewish proselyte baptism and Christian baptism is unacceptable to many who argue for believers' baptism. Ironically enough, the connection, when granted, may promote their cause. W. D. Davies assumes the bond and advises that

> the Jewish treatment of proselytes may enlighten us as to the way in which Paul, and others, dealt with converts to Christianity. Now the process by which a man was made a proselyte was three-fold: it consisted of circumcision, immersion in water (i.e. baptism), and the presentation of an offering in the Temple. Of these rites baptism assumed a growing importance. . . . More-over, from the Rabbinic sources it is clear that the baptism of a proselyte was an occasion of his instruction. . . . It is probable that . . . there was much hortatory and ethical material which every Rabbi used . . . at his own discretion. For our immediate purpose, however, we point out that if, as seems likely, Christian baptism is probably closely related in origin to Jewish proselyte baptism, we should expect it to be the occasion of moral instruction like its counterpart in Judaism.[56]

It is, of course, self-evident that baptism which is an occasion for moral instruction would be a baptism of adults and believers. Prose-lyte baptism did not exclude infants, but for the most part was ad-ministered to adults who were being converted from paganism. Hence the reason for ethical and moral instruction is plain. The preferred and normal form of the rite of baptism had to be modified in the case of infants. It is unlikely that infants were subjected to ethical confrontation and moral instruction.

The scriptural evidence for believers' baptism may now be sum-marized. First of all, the direct references to baptism in the New

[56] W. D. Davies, *Paul and Rabbinic Judaism* (London: S.P.C.K. Press, 1958), p. 121.

Testament are those of adults and presumably believers. This enjoys general agreement. Secondly, the two main interpretations of baptism appearing in the New Testament encourage the doctrine of believers' baptism. The hearing and receiving of the word, which involves faith, is acknowledged as necessary to a valid baptism. The New Testament speaks of faith on the part of the one baptized without ruling out the faith of the baptizing congregation. Nowhere, however, do the scriptures imply that religious corporateness may compensate for the lack of faith on the part of the individual who is baptized. The second interpretation is that of identification. It is couched in terms of such demanding and sacrificial discipleship as to be completely inappropriate for an infant. There is no place for an infant in a baptism which identifies him with Christ, not mystically, but actually into his life and death. The question which Jesus put to James and John is an inquiry reserved only for the mature. And the fact that the choice was left to them indicates that decision on the part of the one to be baptized is essential. Furthermore, the ethical quality of the act connoting a new person with a new moral persuasion militates against the act of infant baptism. An infant is not asked to make moral and ethical choices.

5   The Historical Basis for Believers' Baptism

Whatever confidence the devotees of believers' baptism may have because of biblical testimony is not sustained by a study of history. There is a divergence of opinion as to when infant baptism became the norm for the Church. No one questions the fact that it did become the norm.

Some claim that there were infant baptisms, albeit of isolated incidence, in the first century. Others speak more vigorously for its practice in the second century. Of real interest is what the opponents of infant baptism have to say on the question. Argyle, as was noted, is ready to admit that infant baptism was the normal practice of the Church by the fifth century. If it had become the norm by the fifth century, it is a logical assumption, as Jeremias observes, that the practice had begun some time before. It is conceded that the apostolic tradition of Hippolytus, representing the practice of the Roman Church at the beginning of the third century, makes "provision . . . for the baptism of little children, parents or relatives acting as sponsors," although "the baptism here set forth is mainly that of adult believers." [57]

It is common knowledge that Augustine of Hippo brought to the fourth century a systematic theological structure for the practice of infant baptism. He blamed his mother, who refused to allow his baptism at an early age out of fear of the greater guilt of sin after baptism, for failing to protect him against the pollution and guilt of sin during his earlier years. He believed that baptism in infancy would have been his protection.

No scholar can ignore the huge stockpile of evidence which indicates that relatively soon after New Testament times infant baptism was the prevailing form within the Church. It is also true that there was little or no controversy concerning the practice from the time of its early acceptance until the Reformation. The question was not a major issue during Luther's debate with Rome. The Anabaptists did not raise the issue in their contest with the Reformers until they sought a symbol for the "true church" as they understood it.

Believers' baptism, in whatever was its original form, suffered a virtual eclipse until the advent of the Reformation. Even then it came back into focus not as the central concern of the Anabaptists but as a by-product. Their germinal interest was with the nature and mission of the true church.

"We have to do here with a fundamentally different understanding of the Church and the Christian life. That is why the Anabaptists form an independent Reformation tradition. . . . For the Anabaptists . . . the new life in Christ through the Spirit rather than justification by faith is the center of the New Testament faith and therefore of the Church. The life of the redeemed, the presence of the Spirit in believers, is foremost. Not the Word of God as found in

[57] A. Gilmore (ed.), *Christian Baptism* (London: Lutterworth Press, 1959), chap. 5, "Baptism in the Early Centuries," by A. W. Argyle, p. 203.

the Bible, but the experience of Christ's presence is the foundation of the Church." [58]

The point is far too important to gloss over. The Anabaptists were not initially concerned with baptism. They were enthralled with a Church determined by the presence of the Spirit in the believer. This accent on a spiritual experience inevitably led to the secondary, although important, consideration of the validity of infant baptism.

Theron Price has explained the situation like this:

> From the Anabaptist point of view, the difference between the Reformers and themselves was the difference between reform and restitution. . . . Only the restoration of a church which had, in reality, long since ceased to exist was adequate to God's demand and the need of the times. The Church of Rome—and the Church of the Reformation, insofar as it remained a territorial or parish church—could not vindicate its place in history or be usable in God's scheme. . . . The real problem, therefore, was not the act of baptism but mutually exclusive views of the Church. The difference in interpretation of the "subject" of baptism only served to highlight the irreconcilability of the two views of the Church.[59]

From these Anabaptist revolutionaries may have come the groups which are presently the chief exponents of believers' baptism. Apart from smaller sectarian movements, the leading denominations advocating it are the Baptists and the Disciples. Since the latter are an outcropping of American pluralism, the Baptists' past offers longer historical continuity. Their history would appear to be more advantageous for our study in this regard.

The assumption that Baptists come directly from the Anabaptist movement of the Reformation is not unchallenged by contemporary historians. The *Mennonite Quarterly Review* of October, 1962, pre-

[58] John Dillenberger and Claude Welch, *Protestant Christianity* (New York: Charles Scribner's Sons, 1954), p. 63.

[59] Duke McCall, *What Is the Church?* (Nashville, Tenn.: Broadman Press, 1958), chap. 6, "The Anabaptist View of the Church," by Theron Price, p. 101.

sents two articles of considerable importance on this question.[60] Lonnie Kliever and Glenn Stassen co-operate to offer a credible argument that neither the General Baptists nor the Particular Baptists owe their origins to the Anabaptist movement. In writing on the General Baptists, Kliever declares that Thomas Helwys and the General Baptists of England held a theological position quite distinct from the Mennonite views adopted later by Smyth, who is often called the founder of the first of the Baptist churches: "Every distinctive Mennonite doctrine which Smyth included in either of his confessions of 1609 or 1612 was countered by Helwys—the doctrines concerning rejection of original sin, freedom of the will, analytic view of justification, Hofmannite Christology, the particular concept of the 'gathered church,' the ministry and its exclusive powers, the severity of discipline, the precedence of the New Testament over the Old, and the believer's relation to government, war and oathtaking." [61]

Kliever's main contribution rests with the following observation:

> Too often commentators have seen believers' baptism or the gathered church, or separation of church and state in both the Anabaptist and Baptist traditions, and on this basis uncritically assumed significant theological and historical kinship. However, these doctrines are based on quite different assumptions and hence carry different implications for each group. The determinative distinctive doctrines for these two traditions are original sin, freedom of the will, and justification. Doctrines concerning the Church, good works and society are shaped by the way these prior and more important problems are understood.[62]

The relation of the history of General Baptists to the question of their adoption of believers' baptism is also summed up by Kliever. General Baptists did not borrow their commitment to believers' bap-

---

[60] Lonnie D. Kliever, "General Baptist Origins: The Question of Anabaptist Influence"; Glenn H. Stassen, "Anabaptist Influence in the Origin of Particular Baptists," *Mennonite Quarterly Review* (Mennonite Historical Society, Goshen College, Goshen, Ind.), October, 1962.

[61] *Ibid.,* p. 313.

[62] *Ibid.,* pp. 313-314.

tism but possessed it rather because of "the Reformation understanding of justification by faith, the Puritan view of the sacraments, the Separatist concept of the church composed of believers only in covenant with God and one another, the Separatist conviction that the Established Church was totally corrupt. . . ." [63] One of the moving forces toward believers' baptism was the Baptists' belief that their infant baptism had come at the hands of the Antichrist within the established Church. It is generally conceded that these events occurred during the latter half of the sixteenth century and at the turn of the next. In this period the General Baptists appeared on the scene as a "leftward movement of Puritanism and a logical extension of Separatism." [64]

Stassen asserts that the Particular Baptists began as a party distinct from the General Baptists sometime in the late 1630's. In an article equally striking and persuasive as that of Kliever's, he states his premise: ". . . the Particular Baptists are the fathers of present-day Baptists. Their decision on baptism, and not John Smyth's decision, is the origin 'from which modern Baptists both in England and America have generally sprung.' General Baptists largely died out, trailing off into Unitarianism." [65]

Menno Simon's *Foundation Book* may have occupied a place of prominence in helping to shape the Particular Baptists' doctrine of believers' baptism. To that extent there is a connection between the believers' baptism practiced by the Anabaptist and Particular Baptist tradition. However, this could not be basic. "We are particularly struck with the [Particular] Baptists' lack of concern about the nature of the church. Neither separation from an impure church, nor gathering a pure church, nor constructing a church and an ecclesiology which are special and uniquely Baptist, receives any emphasis." [66] For these Christians, baptism had little meaning as initiation into Christ and the Church. "Death, burial, and resurrection is clearly the central motif of this doctrine of baptism." [67] It is also apparent

[63] *Ibid.,* p. 318.
[64] *Ibid.,* p. 321.
[65] *Ibid.,* p. 322.
[66] *Ibid.,* p. 328.
[67] *Ibid.,* p. 329.

that baptism as profession of faith gripped the minds of early thinkers among the Particular Baptists.

It is still too early to estimate the significance and durability of the trend of thought introduced by these two enterprising young theologians. In the light of this admission the reader has the right to wonder why so much attention has been given to the content of two brief and somewhat untried articles. The attention seems justifiable because this side of the historical Baptist question offers a more comprehensive view of the development of the position of believers' baptism. Coupled with the more accepted view that Anabaptists and Baptists are closely related, the work of Kliever and Stassen offers a wider base from which to view our own special concern.

The difference between the General and Particular Baptists may need a summary clarification. The first group held to a greatly modified Calvinism. The second stayed with Calvin almost to the letter. General Baptists, as has been observed, belonged to the Separatist tradition. The Particular Baptists were more of the non-Separatist category and did not refuse fellowship with members of the Church of England.

The point at which they differed from each other, as Winthrop Hudson observes,

was with regard to their attitude toward the Church of England. The Separatists took what is commonly described as a sectarian position: they contended that the Church of England was a false church and insisted that the break with it must be complete and uncompromising. The non-Separatists were more ecumenical in spirit. They sought to maintain some bond of unity among Christians. They recognized that even the purest churches are subject to mixture and error. Therefore they were unwilling to renounce the Church of England as being utterly corrupt, and thus to separate themselves completely from these Christians who remained with the parish churches.[68]

---

[68] Winthrop Hudson (ed.), *Baptist Concepts of the Church* (Valley Forge, Pa.: Judson Press, 1959), chap. 1, "By Way of Perspective," by Winthrop Hudson, pp. 12-13.

Whatever the original reasons, Anabaptists and General Baptists declared against the Church of their times. While the Anabaptists were doing battle with Luther and Calvin on the continent, General Baptists were disclaiming the authenticity of the Church of England. In these instances, it should not be overlooked that the doctrine and practice of believers' baptism grew out of the doctrines of original sin, freedom of the will, and justification, so far as the Anabaptists and General Baptists were concerned; or, from their concept of the Church itself. In either event baptism was a secondary consideration—almost an afterthought. It was brought in either or both to shore up the doctrines already mentioned or the doctrine of the Church as they understood it. It was not material to the formulation of the doctrine of baptism; rather it was but speculation.

When the Particular Baptists came to the fore, baptism received a somewhat different treatment. Because of their lack of interest in the nature of the Church, the rite was robbed of its initiatory element. By distinction from the General Baptists, for whom baptism was chiefly the means of enrollment, the Particular Baptists showed greater interest in the theological meaning of the act. It became both a confession of faith and a proclamation of God's redemption. The result was that, while believers' baptism gained in theological importance, it lost its significance as Christian initiation.

What happened to baptism in this period of Baptist beginnings is pertinent in a number of ways. It is sufficient for us now to pinpoint the fact that the exclusive, introverted, and non-co-operative General Baptists were more interested in the nature of the Church than they were in baptism. The ecumenical Particular Baptists did not concern themselves too much with the Church, but they were involved with the question of proper baptism as a valid category of concern on its own terms.

It may sound strange that the more ecumenical Baptist movement of the early days was the one which thrived in America. This land watched Baptists grow by the dynamic of finding the people where they were and ministering to them accordingly. This ecumenical spirit could not survive for long before the rapid rise of religious pluralism in the United States. It became ever more necessary to have or to invent some distinctive characteristic which gave to a denomination the right to be. But the structure of Baptist life in America had already been cast. Although it moved to stricter positions on baptism—namely, the baptism of believers by immersion—it had already been influenced by the ecumenical flavor. Even now, Baptists defy the experts. The Baptists of the American Baptist Convention are generally at home with the World Council of Churches and contribute substantially to its life and ministry; furthermore, although Southern Baptists have consistently refused to join ecumenical structures and movements, they remain among the most ecumenical of all religious groups at the local level and in every informal and structureless milieu. When one realizes that the ecumenical Baptists won the day in America before moving to more rigid positions, especially as regards baptism, the paradox is more understandable.

One of the favorite sons of Southern Baptists, prominent during the middle and late nineteenth century, was John A. Broaddus, whose writing on preaching is still among the classics. Broaddus wrote these words for a pamphlet distributed by the American Baptist Publication Society: "We insist that baptism ought to be simply what Christ practiced and commanded. We care nothing for the mode of baptism, the manner of baptizing, if only there is a real baptism according to the plain indications of the scripture." [69]

As recently then as the time of Broaddus the mode of baptism was still an open question. He did not think the matter important. This view, however reflective of the Baptist position in his day, did not survive. Baptists and others of the tradition started sharpening their distinctiveness upon the cut of an exclusive baptism. The baptism which came to be in this manner appears to be similar to that of the New Testament in terms of the form of baptism and its subjects. The similarity to any other aspect of New Testament baptism is not as certain.

[69] Sydnor L. Stealey (ed.), *A Baptist Treasury* (New York: Thomas Y. Crowell Company, 1958), chap. 4, "Distinctive Baptist Principles," "The Duty of Baptists to Teach Their Distinctive Views," by John A. Broaddus, p. 145.

6   The Theological Argument for Believers' Baptism

Karl Barth has emerged as a champion supporter for the theology of believers' baptism. He is a welcome addition to a position which has not been distinguished in America for articulate leadership. His voice is all the more powerful because he does not belong, by virtue of his church membership, to the tradition he upholds. No one may effectively accuse him of tobogganing down the tilted slope of his own theological bias.

Barth believes that the word and work of Jesus Christ are sufficient unto man's salvation. The power of a sacramental act is not dependent upon its secret mystery and its unseen and unnoticed power. Christ wants His saving act "seen, heard, perceived, savoured, understood, considered, and obeyed, by the man who is saved and believes in his salvation. In the most comprehensive manner, it wants to be recognized and experienced." [70]

This sense of a sacrament seen and savored is a lift to the supporters of believers' baptism. God's gift of grace in a sacramental act does not necessarily slip silently into a person's life. The tendency to assume that God's grace is more efficacious if it travels incognito is unwarranted.

It is equally reasonable to suppose that "the sacramental happening in which a real gift comes to man from Jesus Christ Himself is not in fact any less genuine a happening because Christ's word and work on this occasion in this dimension and form, and Christ's power on this occasion, have not a causative or generative, but a cognitive aim." [71] Why Barth cast the generative and cognitive elements into mutually exclusive categories is hard to say. In the light of his total argument, cognition does not replace the causative but is a logical and legitimate partner in the saving enterprise. Speaking of the difference in baptism without cognition and one that is a conscious act, he observes:

[70] Karl Barth, *The Teaching of the Church Regarding Baptism*, trans. E. Payne (London: S.C.M. Press, 1945), p. 28.
[71] *Ibid.*, p. 29.

Baptism without the willingness and readiness of the baptized is true, effectual and effective baptism, but it is not correct; it is not done in obedience, it is not administered according to proper order, and therefore it is necessarily clouded baptism. It must and ought not be repeated. It is, however, a wound in the body of the Church and a weakness for the baptized, which can certainly be cured but which are so dangerous that another presents itself to the Church: how long is she prepared to be guilty of the occasioning of this wounding and weakening through a baptismal practice which is, from this standpoint, arbitrary and despotic? [72]

It is true that Christ may save us without our knowing and our doing. God's grace is not limited to the fact of our knowledge or even our consent. But our conscious and deliberate response to the saving act, our knowing and doing, does not diminish it in any way. In fact it makes the relationship between God and man what is always intended—that man be in the image of God. The image is inextricably connected with man's obedience. Our being made in God's image means that we have a unique relationship with God. Our remaining in that image or recovering it cannot be divorced from the act of obedience. Baptism is of the same nature. What Christ does in baptism is not dependent upon our knowing or our doing. By the same token, our knowing and our doing does not diminish what He does in baptism but complements it and distinguishes it.

The ethical and moral quality of life depends upon cognition. Although man may be saved without his knowledge or consent, he cannot be a disciple without both. Believers' baptism marks the difference between two great religious questions: "What must I do to be saved?" and "Lord, what would you have me do?" The latter belongs unmistakably to the context of believers' baptism.

"The first and foremost contribution of Baptists to the Church Catholic," in Wheeler Robinson's opinion, "is like that of the Hebrew prophets—the essential and primary place of the moral within the religious. The moral change wrought in genuine conversion, the

---

[72] *Ibid.,* p. 41.

personal repentance and faith which are the religious features of that conversion, the open confession which commits the life to a new purpose—these great truths are admirably and forcibly expressed in believers' baptism by immersion, and expressed as no other Church expresses them. All this is New Testament faith and practice." [73]

We need not lavish distinctive praise upon the Baptists in order to appreciate the point that Robinson makes. What is important is that the repentance and faith expressed in believers' baptism is theologically correct and has its origin in the New Testament doctrines.

The ethical note in believers' baptism bids to outweigh all other theological considerations for its supporters. No longer are its scholars content to say that the true church is made up of the regenerate but also—perhaps more so—that it is made up of committed and faithful disciples. So strongly does White feel about this factor that he willingly cast some obstacles in the path of Paul's symbolism of the burial and resurrection motif of baptism. "It is wrong," he contends, "to let the Pauline interpretation of baptism as burial monopolise the exposition of New Testament thought upon this theme: the baptismal bath is the more frequent and more familiar conception. . . . The ethical obligations accepted in baptism become the assumed basis for apostolic counsel, exhortation and warning. And for each New Testament school, amid all the fuller development of its sacramental implications, baptism remains emphatically confessional, a faith-sacrament rightly shared only with those who thereby respond in belief and surrender to the Christian evangel." [74]

7   Development and Motivation

The motives which pulled the Church in two directions away from the Christian baptism of the New Testament are decisive. We are speaking of legitimate motives in which the integrity of the Church

[73] Sydnor L. Stealey (ed.), *A Baptist Treasury* (New York: Thomas Y. Crowell Company, 1958), chap. 4, "Distinctive Baptist Principles," "The Strength and Weakness of the Baptist," by H. Wheeler Robinson, pp. 189-190.
[74] R. E. O. White, *The Biblical Doctrine of Initiation* (Grand Rapids, Mich.: Wm. B. Eerdmans Publishing Co., 1960), pp. 274-275.

and the welfare of persons were uppermost in the minds of those involved in the development of each baptismal tradition. If these motives can be clearly defined, it will be easier to trace the manner in which they were also obscured, as baptism was subsequently subjected to misuse for a variety of expedient reasons.

Infant baptism is motivated by two vital concerns belonging to Judaeo-Christian history. As the Church continued in a world which did not come to its expected and early end, it took on the features of an institution, challenged to perpetuate itself in the world. The prospect of constant evangelism, while preserving the tradition of faith through the existence of the believing community, did not appeal to the best logic of the early Christians. They endeavored instead to bring historical continuity to the Church through the office of infant baptism. It did not seem proper to forgo this provision for the institution of God. The second concern centered on the children of Christian parents. This called for a multiple consideration. That children of Christian parents, having grown up in a Christian home, should be regarded as objects of the saving work of the Church in the same manner as those who were of a pagan persuasion and came to the Church from the outside did not make sense. If contemporary practice is indicative, Christian parents, in the tradition of believers' baptism, may argue to the contrary, but they do consider and treat their children in a different manner from the unbelieving adult who shows no evidence of previous contact with a Christian home or the Church. Not only was it very important to seek an answer to the question of the child's relationship to Christ as contrasted to the pagan's relationship to Christ, but also to the matter of what to do for the child who was growing up in this Christian community. The solidarity of the believing family, the principle of religious corporateness, and the New Testament sense of a believing and covenant community all served to combine Christian efforts toward establishing and maintaining a community in which the infant would be nurtured and challenged to a Christian life. The Church early felt its responsibility for the child and acted accordingly. It assumed the burden of his salvation and his Christian education by an act of mutual love and faith.

Believers' baptism seems to have had three legitimate motives. Firstly, it attacked the growing menace of sacramental magic. In the beginning its attack was not directed at the idea of sacrament as such. As Barth suggests, it sought to prove that a sacrament need not be secret and mysterious in order to be efficacious. It could be seen, known, and understood without diminishing its power. The fear that the people of God were in danger of being His unconscious, indecisive, and inept disciples was surely one of the prime motives for the inception and the establishment of believers' baptism throughout great sectors of the Church. A second concern dealt with the nature of the Church. Christians, who were proper churchmen, had to be responsive, responsible, and spirit-filled. The Church should not recognize as members those who were not accountable, having had no conscious experience with the Spirit. The true Church was made up of believers only. Baptism of these believers, coupled with the history of immersion and Pauline symbolism, added up to the form and practice of believers' baptism. The final motivation was the ethical one. Baptism into Christ and the Church was initiation into a new life of moral dimensions and ethical tone. One died to sin, not only in the sense that it no longer had dominion over his life; he died to the practice of sin. The reintroduction of ethical responsibility to the rite of baptism had much to do with the rise of believers' baptism in the life of the Church.

8   The Irony

This brief summary of the development of the two doctrinal positions on baptism is fraught with irony. Each confesses that baptism does not mean what it has meant and should mean within the life of the Church. This vacuity is a characteristic of the two traditions in question. Despite this fact, there continues to be a fierce debate between the opposing factions as to the nature and practice of proper Christian baptism. If each could point to a history in which the integrity and practice of its particular faith regarding this rite had been zealously guarded, there would be greater justification for the perennial squabble. It is impossible not to suspect that the arguments are part of a façade. Each tradition, while contending fiercely for its superiority to the other, is covering up the fact that it often plays false to its own proclamations. As has been said, it is all the more difficult to write a book on Christian baptism because most resource material is concerned with proving that one distortion of Christian baptism is superior to another.

The importance of baptism to the life of the Church has been declared. Such importance will suffer lack of recognition so long as it is obscured by the subterfuge of baptismal forms brought into being out of expediency. Nor can there be any hope for a solution to the division of the Church over the baptismal controversy until the rite has been recovered in terms of its original and essential integrity.

Chapter Three

THE MISUSE

OF BAPTISM

The nature and circumstances of a person's birth and early years have much to do with his personality development. We have grown accustomed to analysts and counselors, from different professions, who retrace the road of the inner man back to his beginnings. They probe intently for the minute clue. Attention is given to the evidence of that first trauma which cracked, ever so slightly, the foundation of the life under observation. Skilled minds trace along each supporting beam of personality, looking for the revealing flaw.

Under the best of conditions, this is not an easy task. It is made much more difficult because so many individuals have repressed the traumatic episodes in their lives. The task of the analyst is proportionately arduous to the degree that an analysand has covered up the clues to his inner self with an overlay of distortion. His original and real self is hard to uncover.

Becoming a Christian involves new birth. What is necessary to an understanding of an individual is likewise applicable to what is necessary to an understanding of a Christian. The beginning of his Christian life may provide the clues to comprehending what he is now. If these clues are overlaid by suppression and distortion, the, Christian will hardly be able to understand the nature and meaning of his faith. Assuming that baptism symbolizes the new birth as the act of Christian initiation, it is therefore germane to the nature and the circumstances of new life in Christ. At least this one major clue has been repressed or distorted. In turn, Christians and the Church have suffered a separation from their embryonic environment so far as self-understanding is concerned.

This impasse can be resolved only by uncovering those clues which baptism affords for the meaning of the Christian life and the Church. This must first wait, however, upon the recognition that baptism has been distorted through long years of misuse.

The misuse of baptism has taken place in two settings. First of all, there have been serious perversions of Christian baptism as viewed from the New Testament teaching, by each of the traditions which were outlined in Chapter Two. Secondly, these traditions in turn have further distorted, both in faith and practice, the baptisms which they have developed. As a result, the Church and its people have been hurt or confused, or both.

1 The Anabaptists

Certain doctrines and practices of the Anabaptists of the fifteenth and sixteenth centuries illustrate distortion in the first of the above-mentioned categories. In order to see the developing process of misuse, it is necessary to realize the extent to which the New Testament refers to baptism as an inclusive and unifying action. T. C. Smith has compiled a number of scriptures in this regard and accordingly makes helpful comments. Without exception they come from Paul or from letters seeking to represent his mind on the subject. "While his predominant idea of baptism is union with Christ," Smith observes,

> Paul also suggested that baptism is a symbol of the unity of believers in Christ. . . . The special note of Paul in his Ephesian letter is that the Church is the body of Christ. This idea is advanced in Colossians 1:18, but the expansion of this thought is in Ephesians 1:22 ff. As Christ was incarnate historically, so now he is incarnate spiritually in his church, which is his body. In Christ all humanity becomes one. Christ broke down the middle

wall of partition that separated Jew from Gentile and reconciled both unto God in one body by the cross. (Eph. 2:11 ff.) Ephesians 4:5 mentions baptism as one of the marks of the unity of the Christian fellowship.

In the church at Corinth various members prided themselves upon their gifts and each felt that his gift excelled those of the other Christians. In trying to point out the importance of all gifts, Paul used the body and its members as a figure of speech. This "body" is connected with baptism and the Spirit. "For by one Spirit we are all baptized into one body—Jews or Greeks, slaves or free—all were made to drink of one spirit." (I Cor. 12:13.) Here baptism is viewed as the rite which the Spirit uses for binding men into the unity of the Christian fellowship. Baptism becomes the bond of union of believers.[1]

Nowhere in the New Testament is baptism described as an evidence of distinction, excepting the implication that it distinguished the Christian from the world. Granting this important exception, by no stretch of the imagination can anyone interpret baptism as a distinguishing act by which the Church could initiate or justify its present divisions. "One Lord, one faith, one baptism" [2] is a phrase never intended to have been used by a faction of the Church after it had chosen up sides for the denominational game. It was a call to the Church for a unity of hope and faith.

Roland Bainton tells how the Anabaptists changed this: "The Anabaptists (they preferred to call themselves Baptists) had a theory of the Church that necessitated its separation from the State, because they claimed that the Church should be composed only of heartfelt believers of upright life, whereas the State should include the total body of inhabitants in a community. . . . Consequently, State and Church should not coincide. The symbol of the Baptist system was the rejection of infant baptism and the repetition of the rite in adult

---

[1] Duke McCall (ed.), *What Is the Church?* (Nashville, Tenn.: Broadman Press, 1958), chap. 4, "The Doctrine of Baptism in the New Testament," by T. C. Smith, pp. 76-77.
[2] Eph. 4:5.

life, though for the Baptists there was no repetition because infant baptism was no baptism at all but only a dipping in the Romish bath." [3]

In this wise, the Anabaptists seem to have been the first to modify baptism's inclusive and unifying principle. This was possible because they did not start with the question of baptism but rather with the nature of the Church. Since baptism has to do with Christian initiation, there is cause to doubt that the nature of the Church can be debated without concern for the act by which one enters the Church and is incorporated into the body of Christ. Anabaptists, as well as the General Baptists later on, paid little or no attention to this fact. For example, John Smyth, a name of genuine magnitude in the founding of the General Baptists, was instrumental in organizing two Separatist congregations before he came to the conclusion that believers' baptism was true baptism. A congregation at Gainsborough and another at Scrooby were formed in 1606. In 1607, because of persecution, both congregations moved to Amsterdam. Each congregation was first organized on the covenant concept. According to Kliever, it was not until 1609 that Smyth and his followers came to view believers' baptism as true baptism. They then declared their church invalid and reconstituted themselves as a church on the basis of believers' baptism.[4]

This was in line with former Anabaptist practice in which baptism, instead of the means of initiation into the Church, was a sign by which members identified themselves as belonging to the Church. In each instance, division from another expression of the Church had already taken place. The Anabaptists broke with the Church of the Reformation. The General Baptists walking the Separatist line left the Church of England. It is by no means insignificant that the Particular Baptists, beginning with baptism as a point of doctrinal disagreement, did not follow suit and become a Separatist group. We

[3] Roland Bainton, *The Travail of Religious Liberty* (Philadelphia: The Westminster Press, 1951), pp. 60 f.

[4] Lonnie D. Kliever, "General Baptist Origins: The Question of Anabaptist Influence," *Mennonite Quarterly Review* (Mennonite Historical Society, Goshen College, Goshen, Ind.), October, 1962, p. 300.

can only surmise that baptism still connoted unity to the extent that this Baptist group was reluctant to terminate fellowship with other Christians. A note of equal importance is the reminder that Smyth, with his colleagues, came to believers' baptism by way of "two facets of Separatism." The first affirmed that the Church was composed of believers only, who made a personal request for membership and therein agreed to certain requirements. Secondly, it was generally agreed among Separatists and General Baptists that the Church of England was the Antichrist; consequently, those who had been baptized by the Church of England had been baptized by Antichrist. The doctrine and practice of baptism itself was not a point of major concern. The fact that baptism had been administered by a Church and its priests, who were demonic, was the final contributing factor bringing General Baptists to believers' baptism, as had been the case with the Anabaptists before them.[5]

In America, the Particular Baptists showed signs of thriving, while the General Baptists became extinct or drifted off into other religious groups. Under the pressure of a growing religious pluralism, the separatist influence of the General Baptists slowly blended with the baptismal concern and doctrines of the Particular Baptists. As a result, these churches began using the act of baptism as a means to membership in their congregations. Not only converts from the world, but proselytes from other Christian denominations were baptized into local Baptist churches. Believers' baptism evolved gradually but surely into becoming the distinctive differentia of Baptist churches and related churches and groups.

2   Ecumenicity and Mobility

Two other factors in addition to religious pluralism have been instrumental in making baptism a divisive element in organized Christianity. The first is the enduring strength of the ecumenical movement. Despite the fact that Southern Baptist churches, as well as a number of American Baptist and Negro Baptist churches, are not formally connected with the World Council or related ecumenical movements, the ecumenical spirit has worked its leaven within them.

[5] *Ibid.*, pp. 317-318.

Baptists in increasing numbers recognize paedobaptist denominations and churches as being of the Church. Alien immersion and open communion have grown in popularity, especially along the eastern seaboard.

The second factor, sudden and novel in its impact, is the rapidly increasing mobility of American society. Families move from the inner city to the "green belts," from farms to urban areas, and from city to city. Such families are faced with the decision to join a church subsequent to each move. Frequently, the choice is between churches of the same denomination. It is not unusual, however, for the family to cross over from one denomination to another. If, perchance, the parents remain true to their former associations, the children sometimes may leave the church of their parents and become members of a different denomination.

Ecumenicity and mobility have combined to bring about the final transition in the baptismal pilgrimage from a rite of unity and inclusion to one of divisiveness and exclusion. Now we often see churches, such as Baptist, recognizing other churches as authentic and offering their members the rights to full communion, while insisting that they submit to baptism by immersion if they wish to become members of these bodies. The individuals, who are the principals in this strange state of affairs, are told simultaneously that they are both in the Church and not in the Church.

The final result may be clarified by using baptism as a line of demarcation in three stages. In the New Testament stage, baptism marked off the gathered, covenant community from the unbelieving world. It gathered the faithful from out of the world and unified them in the believing community. The second stage, characterized by the Anabaptists and their successors, used baptism chiefly as a means of distinction between what was considered to be the true church and the false church. The act was inserted as the divider between two groups claiming to be Christian, neither of which honored the claim of the other. In the third instance, baptism draws a line of demarcation between categories of the Church which do recognize the validity of one another. It now serves the curious function of distinguishing the "true church" from the "true church." An indi-

vidual may presently be baptized out of the Church of one kind
into the Church of another kind.

Baptism has come a long way from its original setting and purpose.
Once it divided the Church and the world. Now it divides the
churches. No matter what may be argued to the contrary, the present
practice asserts the Anabaptist doctrine. Whenever a Christian from
a recognized church must join another church by baptism, he is
forced to declare, however silently, that his former life in the other
church was totally unauthentic. What the Anabaptists practiced
openly and honestly is now repeated covertly and evasively.

Social mobility has wrought equal confusion within paedobaptist
circles. John Calvin insisted that infant baptism could be justified
only in an educational Christian community. He stoutly contested
the general practice of his day in which a superficial and external
connection with the church was more the rule than the exception.
Schenck helps to outline Calvin's theology and practice in this respect.
"Under the 'Ordonnance of Geneva,' " he explains,

> every member of the church was required to profess his faith in
> Christ and the children of those who made such a profession were
> to be baptized. Calvin, however, by this "ordonnance" did not
> intend to bring his theory into conformity with a current general
> practice of countenancing a merely external connection with the
> church. His purpose was rather to make Geneva, under a the-
> ocracy, such a perfect school of Christ that practice would be raised
> to the level of the ideal conception of the Bible. Only to the
> extent that the ideal of the Bible was realized in the profession
> of faith or baptism of children was there any true religious sig-
> nificance in these rites in the belief of Calvin.[6]

It is not necessary to develop the evident fact that Calvin's experi-
ment at Geneva did not measure up to his expectations. His hope for
a Biblical society of the New Testament variety did not come to
pass. When Geneva did not prove to be the perfect Christian state,

[6] Lewis Bevens Schenck, *The Presbyterian Doctrine of Children in the
Covenant* (New Haven, Conn.: Yale University Press, 1940), pp. 4-5.

Calvin faced the choice of abandoning his cherished dream or of making a workable adjustment to his initial principles. The more it became apparent that he could not populate Geneva with truly committed persons, as he desired, the more he had to modify his original position. He was not willing to follow the course the Anabaptists demanded, namely, that the Church be comprised of regenerated believers only. This would have been the end of infant baptism.

His accommodation at this juncture is classic: "Granting, however, that the church does have many in its number who are not Christians," he conceded, "yet it is likewise true that she should not receive anyone into the church except those who presumably are Christians. Our judgment then must be a judgment of charity. We must take the position that those who profess their personal Saviour are presumably Christians. Likewise, we must accept the children of believing parents as presumably God's children, on the basis of the covenant promise of God. One is certainly no less a ground for assurance than the other. In either case those who enter the church on these grounds are presumably God's own children." [7]

Our present concern is not with Calvin's main contention. Obviously, he sought some kind of consistency by claiming that it was no greater strain to presume that infants of believing parents could be baptized into the Church presumably on the same basis on which the profession of faith made by their parents was accepted. Of more interest for us is that Calvin deserted his first principle, on which infant baptism was justified in his own eyes. That principle was that the infant should be baptized into a community based on faith. He skirted this central issue with a "judgment of charity."

Calvin's moderation of the principle of the necessity of a community of faith being proxy for the faith of an infant has been carried to an untenable extreme in the present day. His acceptance of a decidedly imperfect community paved the way for the further acceptance of an unstable community brought on by the mobility of society. For example, it is common practice for a Presbyterian church to charge a congregation with responsibility at an infant's baptism which the congregation cannot possibly fulfill. The responsibility that

[7] *Ibid.*, p. 11.

the congregation accepts on such an occasion reads as follows: "This child is now received into Christ's Church: And you the people of this congregation in receiving this child promise with God's help to be his sponsor to the end that he may confess Christ as his Lord and Saviour and come at last to His eternal kingdom. Jesus said, 'Whoso shall receive one such little child in my name receiveth me.' " [8]

The response to this charge may not demand a Geneva-like community. It does demand a stable community in which those who accept the charge will remain long enough to fulfill their commitments. A seemingly plausible argument that a congregation may assume the responsibility for the baptized infant on behalf of the entire Presbyterian Church falls under the weight of two observations. First of all, it is the local congregation that is charged with sponsoring the care of the child. Secondly, the parents of an infant, who are planning to move to another city and church, will usually arrange for the baptism of their offspring before they depart. This indicates their own desire to place upon the local congregation, in which they have their friends, the burden of Christian nurture.

Despite the need for a community which will be both faithful and stable in order to validate the baptism of an infant, paedobaptists of Presbyterian and related communions have done little to alter their usual practice. Although because of these changing conditions, infant baptism cannot possibly mean what it once meant, the traditional pattern is still in effect. Borrowing again from Calvin's "judgment of charity," we can only presume that infants under these circumstances have been baptized at all. And this presumption is to be drawn against the doctrine and the practice which the paedobaptists themselves have established and developed.

3   Isolation of Baptism From Its Original Setting

One of the pronounced differences within Anglicanism at the present time highlights a baptismal distortion which occurred before

[8] *The Book of Common Worship* (Philadelphia: The Westminster Press [The Board of Christian Education of the Presbyterian Church, U.S.A.], 1946), p. 123.

the day of John Calvin or the Anabaptists. The debate in question centers around the sacramental nature of confirmation.

Dom Gregory Dix, well known for his study of ancient liturgy, lays considerable store by the "apostolic tradition" of St. Hippolytus. He believes that Hippolytus recorded, among early accounts, the most complete liturgy for Christian initiation. From this record, Dix first draws the conclusion that the norm of New Testament baptism was the immersion of responsible and believing adults. Secondly, he emphasizes that the rite of initiation was offered to catechumens, which implies that the candidates were instructed in the faith, and that profession of faith, immersion in water, and confirmation— which mediated the gift of the Spirit—were the common elements of a single act. In short, profession, baptism, and confirmation were combined under one title—baptism.[9] Taking his cue from this ancient tradition, Dix believes that the separation between the two elements of baptism, water and the Spirit, was first an abnormal practice devised to meet a practical difficulty, and evolved gradually into the normal liturgy.[10]

In consequence, the Anglican liturgist levels some direct and telling blows at the current trends in the Anglican Church that make confirmation a secondary rite that is nonsacramental and not needed in order to complete baptism in any sense whatsoever. ". . . Christian Initiation," he contends,

> in the New Testament is described and conceived of solely in terms of a conscious adherence and response to the Gospel of God, that is solely in terms of an adult Initiation. This must needs raise questions about our present practice. As the Convocation Committee remarks, "It is infant Baptism rather than adult Confirmation which needs justification." It is true that infant Baptism, accompanied always by infant Confirmation, goes back to the second century, probably to the first. . . . I am not suggesting that we should go back on all that. . . . The Church can very well

[9] Dom Gregory Dix, *The Theology of Confirmation in Relation to Baptism* (London: Dacre Press: Adams and Charles Black, 1946), pp. 12-13.
[10] *Ibid.,* p. 21.

afford infant Baptism, even as the practice in the vast majority of
cases (which it never was in pre-Nicene times) provided that it is
never allowed to be thought of as normal, that it is regarded always as an abnormality, wholly incomplete by itself and absolutely
needing completion by the gift of the Spirit and the conscious response of faith for the full living of the Christian "eternal life" in
time.[11]

Many of Dix's colleagues are anything but passive before his open
confession that infant baptism is always an abnormality. They cor-
rectly perceive that Dix makes the confirmation sacrament of equal
import, if not of superior value, to the sacrament of baptism. Furthermore, his suggested completion of infant baptism, in part by a conscious response of faith at the time of confirmation, constitutes a
doctrinal affront to the former rite. It is not necessary to settle the
family argument between Dix and his counterparts in order to
reassert the important fact that the rite has changed from a single
service to one of separated parts.

Concerning the status of confirmation, one opponent of Dix does
agree that the separation between baptism and confirmation was an
unfortunate expedient. G. H. W. Lampe suggests:

It is in the third century that there begins to set in a disintegration both of the New Testament doctrine of the seal and of the
primitive liturgical pattern. It was then that to the effects of the
general adoption of the rites of unction and consignation, the influence of the supposed teaching of Acts about the laying on of
hands, and the tendency to associate the ancient conception of
the covenant-seal with a visible signing with the Cross instead of
with the state of belonging to Christ and so of possessing His
Spirit, there were added the growth of the Church (making it impossible, especially in Rome, for the bishop to remain the sole
regular minister of Baptism), and some unfortunate consequences
of the controversy on rebaptism. These last factors contributed

[11] *Ibid.*, pp. 37-38.

heavily to the development of a separation between Baptism and the secondary rite which came to be regarded as the sacrament of Confirmation, with a corresponding divorce between Baptism and the sacrament of remission of sins and regeneration and Confirmation as the outward sign of the bestowal of the Spirit.[12]

The time lag between baptism and confirmation occurred for two reasons. The first cause was an expedient one. Missionaries, with power to baptize but not to confirm, carried the gospel to remote areas to which there was little likelihood of their returning. The choice was often between infant baptism or no baptism at all. These missionaries chose to baptize infants who were to await confirmation by the proper cleric, who would authenticate and complete that baptism. A second reason is theological in nature. Based on the expediency of the first cause, confirmation grew in stature because it inserted the missing note of mature professional and adult responsibility. Ultimately, it achieved stature within its own right, and its separation from infant baptism was endorsed as more than a corrective for the abnormal rite; it was believed to possess an intrinsic value of its own.

The resulting dilemma for paedobaptist churches is self-evident. If confirmation is as indispensable to complete baptism as Dix warrants, then the rite of infant baptism cannot represent the prevenient grace of God, the gift of the Spirit, and full initiation into Christ and His Church. Confirmation, as a sacrament, poses a definite threat to the sacramental power of infant baptism. On the other hand, if confirmation is not sacramental and serves as the recognition and acceptance of what has already fully come to pass, the New Testament emphasis upon deliberate and responsible decision, as well as upon conscious adherence to the Gospel, is excised from the baptismal rite. Anglicanism is a prime example of the paedobaptist complex. The choice between one of two abnormalities is not a pleasant prospect. If infant baptism is complete and whole within itself, confirmation is an abnormality. If confirmation completes,

---

[12] G. H. W. Lampe, *The Seal of the Spirit* (New York: Longmans, Green & Co., Inc., 1951), p. 153.

fulfills, and corrects infant baptism, then infant baptism is an abnormality. The present strife concerning all such communions is only the logical, inevitable result.

Continuing to take our cue from the liturgy of Hippolytus, we find that the practice of believers' baptism has also altered the earliest baptismal forms. To all intents and purposes, profession of faith has been separated from baptism. This is a much later operation than that reflected in the Anglican complication. The full force of this trend came to pass under the aegis of the "Great Awakening," when revivalism fired the American frontier. Admittedly, the underlying causes of this division are hard to uncover. It has already been pointed out that the Anabaptist movement did not start with a concern primarily for the nature of baptism, but with a concern for the nature of the true church. Therefore, since most of the converts to Anabaptism had been baptized as infants, the accent fell upon belief and profession of faith rather than upon baptism. In the endeavor to rid the act of magic connotations, baptism was given secondary status to the act of belief or faith. This emphasis has prevailed in the tradition of believers' baptism up to the present. Nowhere could it have found more fertile ground than in the revivalist movements of America.

It is evident that confession has no place in infant baptism. Very likely the Anabaptists and their successors would have restored confession to believers' baptism had they come to the fore. This happy prospect did not come to pass. Confession of sin and profession of faith, instead of being coincident with baptism, became its necessary prerequisites. They had to be completed before baptism could be administered. The confessional element was lost to baptism under these conditions in much the same way that confirmation disappeared in the paedobaptist maneuver.

This tragic loss was compounded when the gospel came to America. As soon as the battle for religious freedom was won, wandering evangelists preached on the frontier. They emphasized an emotion-packed, highly subjective response to an "altar call," or "invitation hymn." Baptism was reduced to a formality. It could be easily postponed or dispensed with altogether as far as salvation was concerned. "Getting saved" was the only thing that really mattered. Manifestations of the gift of the Spirit, commonly associated with the act of baptism, were now evidenced in ecstatic gestures, speaking in strange tongues, in cataleptic states, and in other incredible aberrations. The water was emptied of the Word.

Believers' baptism in its usual form of immersion faced even more practical difficulty than did infant baptism. Where infant baptism suffered because of the absence of properly ordained ecclesiastics, believers' baptism suffered from the lack of sufficient and conveniently located water. Also, the water was often too cold in the wintry months. And those hardy souls who remember their baptism in water, to which access was gained by breaking the cover of ice, do not seem to be better Christians despite the rigors of the immersion that they underwent for their faith.

As the churches became more sophisticated and commodious, lighted and heated baptistries were the fashion. Whatever contributed to the time lag between the profession of faith and baptism in more primitive settings was not remedied by the modern conveniences of light and heat. Baptism is postponed in contemporary churches until a reasonable number of candidates is available. This presumably justifies the trouble incurred in filling the pool, as well as the payment of the water bill. More seriously, the desire for a "spectacular" appears as the chief reason.

In any event the important step has already taken place. It is yet possible that a baptismal service on Sunday night will swell the number in attendance. This is the exception rather than the rule. Those professing their faith in Christ usually make a public declaration on Sunday morning. They are greeted, welcomed, and congratulated by the comparatively large congregation. From two to four weeks later they will be baptized, ordinarily on Sunday night, before a yawning few who may have already forgotten their names. A full doctrinal transmutation has taken place. The subjective "I believe," which is frequently no more than walking to the front of the sanctuary and shaking the minister's hand, is of greater significance than the objective act of baptism. The latter has been reduced to the lowest common denominator.

It would be well for all churches involved in these practices to consider that "from the first, and increasingly as time passed, baptism was intimately bound with the confessional aspects of the church's life; it prompted and helped to mould the creeds because it gave birth to them, and because it was the occasion of the teaching of new converts in the essentials of the faith, and even more because baptism is (and had been in Judaism) by its very nature an affirmation of faith, the essentially confessional rite of initiation into an essentially confessional church." [13]

One should balance his emphasis on the confessional nature of baptism by hastening to add that baptism is more than a confession of faith. This is an apt warning. However, the question is not one of more or less, but something else. Baptism is not something other than confession.

The end result of the time lag between confirmation and baptism on one hand and between profession and baptism on the other is an unfortunate one. Baptism is denied the central and dramatic setting for the gift of the Spirit. Not only does this pose theological positions which are not borne out by the New Testament; it also robs baptism of most of its potential. If the baptism of the Spirit is much closer to confirmation than to infant baptism, then the latter rite is a piece of anemic sentimentality. If the baptism of the Spirit is closer to profession of faith than to baptism, then the latter is placid water, never troubled with the birth of new life and too little agitated to be a cleansing flow.

4 Martin Luther

Not only has baptism suffered the loss of confession and confirmation from its earlier structure, but it has also been subjected to frequent changes centering around the question of the locus of its element of faith. Luther proved to be a prime manipulator of these kinds of modifications.

In 1520, addressing himself to Roman Catholic criticism, he said: "Baptism truly saves in whatever way it is administered, if only it

[13] R. E. O. White, *The Biblical Doctrine of Initiation* (Grand Rapids, Mich.: Wm. B. Eerdmans Publishing Co., 1960), p. 153.

be not administered in the name of man but of God. Nay, I have no doubt that if one received baptism in the name of the Lord, even though the wicked minister should not give it in the name of the Lord, he would yet be truly baptized in the name of the Lord. For the effect of baptism depends not so much on the faith or use of him that confers it as on the faith or use of him that receives it." [14]

In this instance, Luther locates the effect of baptism in the subject that is being baptized. The administration of baptism and its administrator is of no significance. Luther's emphasis upon the faith of the candidate is a clear-cut argument for believers' baptism. No wonder that Zwingli could embrace believers' baptism and discount the baptism of infants without anticipating his colleague's irate reaction. If this were all that Luther had said, it would put him in the camp of those clamoring for believers' baptism. But the Reformer took this stand in order to combat the power of the Roman hierarchy. He rendered the entire priesthood of the Roman Catholic Church impotent to weaken baptism's effectiveness.

At the same time, his answers to the Anabaptists were the reverse of his polemic with the Roman Catholics:

. . . some will perhaps point to the baptism of infants, who do not grasp the promise of God and cannot have the faith of baptism; so that either faith is not necessary or infant baptism is without effect. Here I say what all say: Infants are aided by the faith of others, namely, those who bring them to baptism. For the Word of God is powerful when it is uttered to change even a godless heart, which is no less deaf and helpless than any infant. Even so the infant is changed, cleansed, and renewed by inpoured faith, through the prayer of the Church that presents it for baptism and believes, to which prayer, all things are possible. Nor should I doubt that even a godless adult might be changed, in any of the sacraments, if the same Church prayed and presented him. . . . [15]

[14] Martin Luther, *Luther's Works,* trans. John W. Doberstein (Philadelphia: Muhlenberg Press, 1959), LI, 176.
[15] *Ibid.,* p. 187.

Although Luther is not noted for his theological consistency, these two quotations betray an incredible contradiction. To the Anabaptists, Luther was unwilling to yield a single concession. Reversing himself completely, he dared to say that the faith of the individual receiving baptism is of no moment; what really counted was the prayer and belief of the Church which presented the infant for its baptism.

Some eight years later, when he was apparently pressed on the issue, Luther reaffirmed infant baptism with the following note:

Note well, therefore, that baptism is water with the Word of God, not water and my faith. My faith does not make the baptism but receives the baptism, no matter whether the person being baptized believes or not; for baptism is not dependent upon my faith but upon God's word. If today a Jew were to be baptized, who was seeking only the sponsor's Christening gift, and we baptized him nevertheless, the baptism would be genuine, for it is God's Word with water. And even though the Jew did not believe, the baptism would nevertheless not be false. . . . Therefore, it is false to say that infants do not believe and therefore should not be baptized. You have already heard that they do believe, because the fruits follow, namely, the gift of the Holy Spirit. Even if the children did not believe, which, however is false, the baptism is not to be repeated. Therefore, you should say: The Baptism was genuine, but I, unfortunately, did not believe it.[16]

By this time, Luther had introduced two additional thoughts speaking for the effectiveness of baptism. The first was that baptism is the work and word of God to which faith is an unnecessary appendage. Secondly, he decided that in the final analysis the infant does have faith at baptism. The matter became still more confused when Luther said that if one makes the mistake of failing to believe that the infant had faith at his baptism, he should not be forced to a second baptism later on. The unbelieving adult or congregation might then confess that the baptism was proper but that there was an un-

[16] *Ibid.*, pp. 186-187.

fortunate lack of faith by those witnessing it. Note well the circle in which Luther has traveled. In the chronological sequence in which he has been quoted, he starts with the faith of the candidate as the most essential element in baptism. In the setting in which he declared this, everything points to the faith of a mature believer. His next step is the claim that the faith and prayers of the Church, the administrator, are the indispensable factors in effective baptism. In the third instance, baptism is the Word of God with water, and its power is dependent upon God's Word and not the faith of the person baptized. Lastly, he attributes an efficacious faith to the infant who is baptized.

Anticipating that some readers may rush to Luther's defense, it is admitted that the foregoing is not all that he had to say about baptism. This much he did say, however, and there is no assurance that a consistent note would be found if every utterance he made about baptism were listed. In a manner similar to the Anabaptists, whom he violently deplored, Luther was concerned to establish and defend his understanding of the nature of the Church. In single-mindedly devotion to that end, he revealed a flexible mind with regard to baptism. There can be no question but that he was guilty of distorting its doctrines and that he was not reluctant to approach the subject with pragmatic motives.

Luther's sincerity in defending his position on the nature of the Church is beyond question. This does not justify, however, the degree to which baptism suffered because of his mistaken positions. Johannes Schneider quotes from one of the Reformer's sermons what may have been the latter's basic position on the rite, as well as the one most tolerable to himself. Luther said: "Without personal faith no one should be baptized. Where we cannot be sure that young children are themselves believers and themselves have faith, my advice and judgment are that it is better to delay, and even better that we baptize no more children, so that we do not with such folly and tricks make a mockery of or outrage the blessed majesty of God!" [17]

It is to Luther's credit that he wrestled as few men have with the

[17] Johannes Schneider, *Baptism and Church in the New Testament* (London: Carey Kingsgate Press, Ltd., 1957), p. 11.

problem. He wished with real fervor, no doubt, that baptism remain "untouched and untainted" by men. His love for the sacrament of baptism could not, in the last analysis, match his love for the Church as he understood it. He realized that the Reformation movement would have difficulty finding sufficient manpower without the aid of infant baptism. As much as any other man of the Church, he is vulnerable to Barth's phlegmatic and sharply critical observation: "Am I wrong in thinking," Barth asks rhetorically,

> that the really operative extraneous ground for infant-baptism, even with the Reformers, and ever again quite plainly since, has been this: one did not want then in any case or at any price to deny the existence of the evangelical Church in the Constantinian corpus christianum—and today one does not want to renounce the present form of the national church? If she were to break with infant baptism, the Church would not easily any longer be a people's church in the sense of a state church or a church of the masses. . . . Has not the anxiety, which here shows itself, often unconsciously the quite primitive form to which Luther openly confessed on occasion; there would not be too many people baptized, if instead of being brought to baptism, they had to come of their own accord.[18]

5   Christian Baptism in the Fight for Proper Church Doctrine

Although the Roman Catholic doctrine of baptism does not, in a major sense, fall within the scope of this book, we must look at it briefly for the sake of our over-all purpose. Our concerns will best be served by a glance at the Roman Catholic Church's view of its relationship to the Holy Spirit.

In the Roman view, the Church is primarily the successor of Christ; the presence and power of the Holy Spirit are then re-

[18] Karl Barth, *The Teaching of the Church Regarding Baptism*, trans. E. Payne (London: S.C.M. Press, 1945), pp. 52-53.

garded as endowments bequeathed by Christ to the Church to enable it to discharge its supernatural role. . . . Two things are noteworthy about this conception. The disciples are viewed exclusively in the role of successors to Christ; his mission, which is left incomplete by him at his departure, devolves upon them. . . . The other feature of Roman Catholic theory which should be noted is this. In the assumption that the mission of Christ is transmissible to his disciples, there is an implicit denial of the completeness and finality of the work of Christ, and, with that, a loss of its evangelical character; for what makes the gospel truly gospel is the fact that "it is finished"; God's decisive deed for the salvation of the world is done once for all and nothing needs to be added to it.[19]

Commensurate with this interpretation, George Hendry proceeds to his conclusion,

that in the Roman Catholic view the Holy Spirit fulfills a purely instrumental role in establishing a direct continuity between Christ and the Church. There is no place in the Roman Catholic system for a confrontation of the Church with the Holy Spirit as Lord, i.e., as witness to the Lordship of Christ over the Church. Rather, the Holy Spirit, as the soul of the Church, is the source from which the Church is inflated by its own authoritarian claim. . . . In Roman Catholic theology the chief interest is always in the effects of the Holy Spirit, the gifts and graces that spring from his indwelling; the Holy Spirit is thought of as an impersonal principle, a source or channel of supernatural endowments, rather than a Lord and a Person.[20]

In essence, because the Roman Catholic Church does not distinguish between itself and the Risen Lord, it assumes the custody of the Holy Spirit. Its doctrine of baptism has arisen out of these pre-

[19] George Hendry, *The Holy Spirit in Christian Theology* (Philadelphia: The Westminster Press, 1956), pp. 55-57.
[20] *Ibid.*, p. 58.

conceived opinions of the Church. As custodian, the Church gives the
Spirit to whomever it baptizes. Even an infant is made sinless by the
regenerating gift of the Spirit at the hands of the Church. Baptism
and salvation are synonymous.

"All Catholic errors," in Reinhold Niebuhr's opinion, "in over-
estimating the sinlessness of the redeemed, reach their culmination,
or at least their most vivid and striking expression, in the doctrine
of the church. Here the reservations of Augustine are forgotten; and
the church is unreservedly identified with the Kingdom of God. . . .
The edification of the church is spiritually dangerous, however conceived. The Catholic doctrine that the church is an 'extension of the
Incarnation' represents a significant shift of emphasis from the
Pauline-Biblical doctrine that the church is the 'body of Christ.' " [21]
The church in question here commits the error of forgiving "sins"
instead of "sinners." Its baptism serves as a "magic wash," cleansing
the person of every spot and stain. A major contribution of Reformation theology consisted of a trend away from magical baptism
and to "justification by faith" for those who were still in their sins.

The evangelical-Protestant understanding of the relation between
the Holy Spirit and the Church, to which we now turn, is determined primarily by its concern for the integrity of the gospel. . . .
The fundamental objection of the Roman Catholic position is
that it destroys the gospel by obliterating any distinction between
the gospel and the teaching of the Church. In Roman Catholicism,
as we have seen, the Church is to all intents and purposes the
successor of Christ; it has inherited from him, through the apostles,
"the same mission and the same mandate which he had received
from the Father," and it has been endowed with the power of the
Holy Spirit to enable it to fulfill it. . . . The heart of the Protestant position is found in its conception of what may be called the
abiding polarity between Christ and the Church. . . . According
to the New Testament, the mission of Christ does not require to be
taken over, for it is complete; what he accomplished is sufficient

[21] Reinhold Niebuhr, *The Nature and Destiny of Man* (New York: Charles
Scribner's Sons, 1949), Part I, pp. 144-145.

for all. It requires only to be communicated to men; and this is the primary responsibility laid upon the apostles.[22]

In opposition to a Church identical with the Gospel and with Christ, Hendry proposes a Church to which the Risen Lord proclaims the Gospel through His Spirit. The apostles do not carry on the work of Christ. Nor does the Church. Christ continues His redemptive ministry in the Spirit. It is the responsibility of the Church to provide a consistent witness to the ongoing redemptive work of a living Christ.

Having clarified the relation between the Church and the Spirit, the Reformers were left with the problem of the connection between water-baptism and spirit-baptism. Roman Catholics had encountered no difficulty here, since they taught that the Church gave the spirit to those whom it baptized at the time the rite was administered. When the theologians of the Reformation wrested the Spirit's custody from the ecclesiastical control of the Roman Church, they were forced to find another medium for the Holy Spirit and its work. This ultimately constituted a search for some other authority than the Church. At the end of this search was the Bible. Gradually, with the authority given to the written scriptures, the Holy Spirit became inextricably involved with the Holy Book.

"The Reformation insistence upon the authority of Scripture, as against the authority of the church, bears within it the perils of a new idolatry. Its Biblicism became, in time, as dangerous to the freedom of the human mind in searching out causes and effects as the old religious authority." [23] Here Niebuhr puts a finger on the Reformation's trend toward the eventuality of a "bibliolatry." The Book which Luther had called the "cradle of Christ" developed into the incarceration of the Spirit. The Church looked to the Bible for its authority, and baptism's validity was determined solely in accordance with the scriptures. The rite was ultimately reduced to that act by which the Church enrolled its members. Dillistone reminds us that the "ceremony came all too easily to be regarded as the necessary

[22] Hendry, *op. cit.*, pp. 63-64.
[23] Niebuhr, *op. cit.*, p. 152.

and recognized sign of admission into Church membership and the richer and deeper notes in the original symbolism were either overlaid or lost." [24]

Baptism as the means of enrollment by the Church bore too great a resemblance to the Roman Catholic sacrament. Recognizing the need for a regenerate membership and the relation between baptism and faith, Luther was forced to conclude, as we have seen, that infants were capable of having faith.

The third main division of the Church, in this historic retrospect, was primarily initiated by the Anabaptists and those sects which arose partly as the result of Anabaptist influence. These latter were comprised of pietistic groups, which believed in the perfection of individual life, and radical social movements, which sought a perfect society. Christian authority went through a process of introversion so far as the pietist segments were concerned. Man need look only to his inner self and find that authority dwelt inwardly where the Spirit had entrenched itself. The Spirit was no longer domesticated by the Roman Catholic Church nor imprinted upon an inflexible page. It enjoyed a sovereign and inviolate freedom, so much so that it came to be an entity within itself. The pietist—or enthusiast, to use Hendry's word—not only freed the Spirit from the Church and Bible, but almost separated the Spirit from Jesus Christ.

"The real attitude of enthusiasm," Hendry insists,

is that the dispensation of the Spirit superseded the historical revelation of Christ. This is concealed in modern forms of enthusiasm beneath an appearance of devotion to the Christ of the New Testament, but it is not really changed; for the historical revelation of Christ is treated as a stimulus to a subjective spiritual experience in the individual, not as itself the content of that experience. The spiritualist individual experiences his own conversion and the resultant spiritual glow rather than Jesus Christ and him crucified; when he bears his testimony, it is to speak of his new-

---

[24] F. W. Dillistone, *Christianity and Symbolism* (Philadelphia: The Westminster Press, 1955), p. 202.

found peace and happiness rather than to confess that Jesus Christ is Lord.[25]

In the wake of the Reformation adjustment (which, in its endeavor to correct the magical element in Roman Catholic baptism, reduced the act to church enrollment), the pietist and Anabaptist movements of necessity severed their ties to the Church altogether. The break between water-baptism and spirit-baptism was complete. The Spirit's visitation not only was conceived as antecedent to baptism but was thought to have "superseded the historical revelation of Christ." Baptism had become a sign, somewhat artificial and contrived, which was to be laid upon those who were already of the Church. Their membership in the Church was not so much on the basis that they had been gathered under the Lordship of Christ, but on the basis that they had had a personal experience with the Spirit. Baptism's contribution to the "objective thereness" of the Gospel was no longer important. As the Spirit had led Jesus to be baptized, so the Spirit led these Christians to the same ceremony. In their compliance they were following Jesus and obeying what He commanded. Furthermore, as time progressed, artistically horrendous pictures of the river Jordan appeared on the back walls of the baptismal pools to create the impression that the candidates were being baptized as much like Jesus was as possible.

These three divisions of the Church have one thing in common. Each determined for itself the nature of the Church apart from baptism's conscience or clue. It does not follow that the doctrine of baptism must be initially ascertained before the nature of the Church may even be contemplated. But we must not forget that baptism was originally "into Christ." Nor is it now possible to separate "being in Christ" from being in the Church. Therefore, the means by which the Church offers the act of Christian initiation and enrollment into itself will have unmistakable bearing upon what the Church will be in the final analysis.

[25] George Hendry, *The Holy Spirit in Christian Theology* (Philadelphia: The Westminster Press, 1956), pp. 68-69.

Chapter Four

THE ABUSE OF

BAPTISM AND

ITS PRACTICAL RESULTS

The foregoing attempts to uncover baptismal abuses in the Church's history may claim only partial success. Because they do not lend themselves to explicit documentation in every instance, they are liable to criticism. Without other means for underscoring evident abuses, our major premise would be forced to stand in a defenseless position, since the history of baptism is overlaid with obscure and ambiguous elements.

The contemporary setting is more amenable environment for definitive illustrations. The two major baptismal traditions are not as completely concealed from the watchful eye of present observers as they were from those of earlier years. The baptismal distortions for which they are responsible are revealed in their practical consequences, which result from former deviations. It is upon such tangible, specific material that considerable reliance may be placed in achieving our purpose.

Although this procedure demands unflinching frankness, the promise of rewarding discoveries alleviates the burden of candor. In the study of baptismal distortions and their practical results, we may return to Christian baptism and its good effects.

1   Procedure

The plan for this effort is a simple one. The connection between infant baptism and the "church-type" Church, along with the connection between believers' baptism and the "sect-type" Church, will be utilized as a working premise. This will be followed by a study of the effects of baptismal distortion upon the institutional Church of our day. Finally, both infant and believers' baptism will be observed in their relationship to evangelism, Christian education, worship, and ecumenicity.

2   Church and Sect

William Hordern makes good use of Troeltsch's descriptive definitions of the two types of Church. He reminds us that "the sect, according to Troeltsch, is that type of Christianity which arose from time to time to insist that the Christian had to be different from society, that the Church must include only the saints. . . . Sects believed that the Church had broken faith with the New Testament by becoming assimilated to the world. Adult baptism was the symbol frequently used to represent their belief that one could not enter the fold until he was mature enough to make a decision for Christ and to be a practicing Christian." [1]

As has been implied, this provides a workable view of those groups belonging to the tradition of believers' baptism. No claim is made that this is an exhaustive description. It suffices for the purpose at hand. Our concern is whether the overriding principle behind believers' baptism, expressed in the "sect-type" Church, is maintained by those Christians who stoutly proclaim in its behalf. The obvious way to test the principle is to see whether it persists in the Church at work—in evangelism, Christian education, worship, and ecumenical pursuits.

The Church is that form of Christian organization which does not limit its membership to the "saints"! It recognized that the redeemed man is also a sinner and did not believe that there

[1] William Hordern, *Christianity, Communism and History* (Nashville, Tenn.: Abingdon Press, 1954), pp. 16-17.

could be a society of the perfect. As a result it did not try to withdraw from society, but rather remained in it, hoping that it could do more to change society from within than it could by an exclusive withdrawal. The Church hoped to include all the persons in a given area, receiving them by baptism while they were infants. This meant that the Church was ever in danger of losing the full Christian witness. It became so adjusted to the world that it forgot that it was an outpost of heaven.[2]

As was true of the first definition, this is an oversimplification. The Church was no more casual about enrolling saints than the sect was blind in believing that it possessed only the saints. The sect did not completely withdraw from the world, nor was the Church wholly absorbed by it. But, again, the definition serves as a workable base for our purpose. The question here is similar to the preceding one: Did the overriding principle of infant baptism in the "church-type" Church persist to the degree that its advocates proclaimed?

The moderating influence of a church historian may well be brought to bear upon these questions and their answers. A. H. Newman wisely asks yet another question:

> Was there, then, a failure of the assurance of Christ that the gates of Hades should not prevail against his church? Far be it! We are not able to prove, it is true, that from the close of the apostolic age to the twelfth century a single congregation existed that was in every particular true to the apostolic norm; but that there were hosts of true believers even during the darkest and most corrupt periods of Christian history does not admit a doubt. That a church may make grave departures in doctrine and practice from the apostolic standard without ceasing to be a church of Christ must be admitted, or else it must be maintained that during long periods no church is known to have existed.[3]

[2] *Ibid.*, p. 17.
[3] A. H. Newman, *Baptists.* Vol. II of the American Church History Series (New York: The Christian Literature Co., 1894), p. 13.

Newman's reminder is propitious. It ought to be added, however, that, since the twelfth century, as well as before, it would be hard to find a congregation which has "been true in every particular to the apostolic norm."

Newman's observation is not intended to soften some of the realities to be uncovered in answer to the above questions. It does stage these answers in their proper perspectives. The reality of the Church depends neither upon the rightness of paedobaptists nor on their antagonists. This is the responsibility of Christ and He fulfills it.

3   Institutionalism

The Church is an institution. The lament of spiritual sentimentalists notwithstanding, the Church is a Christian organization from which no major characteristic of an institution is missing. If the Church of our time is to be criticized, it must be criticized as an institution rather than because it is one. Sectarian deviations from the main stream of religious institutionalism are no longer the mark of the impoverished and dispossessed, who fervently hope to get their institutional privileges in heaven. Intellectuals, freethinkers, social liberals, and iconoclasts represent small and intense religious reactions against conformity. This is both helpful and exciting. But sooner or later, men either grow tired of the mere negation of institutionalism or move on with increased despair when they discover that they, too, have been institutionalized. In this light we look at baptism and the institutional Church of the day.

The plight of paedobaptists' institutions may be introduced by the observation of Clarence Tucker Craig. Registering dismay at the nominal quality of membership in the churches of this persuasion, he writes: "A whole series of factors has contributed to the bringing of this issue to the forefront. The first is an increasing awareness of the anomaly of a situation where millions of baptized persons have no active relation with the Church. Baptism is something which has happened to them but not of their own seeking. Their lives correspond in no way to what is said about the nature of the Church.

The number is largest where there is a state church and practically all of the population are baptized." [4]

Factual evidence underscoring Craig's concern comes from a typical statistic: "According to a recent report, the sum of baptized Anglicans in two populous English church provinces, Canterbury and York, was 26,700,000, but of this number only 9,600,000 had also been confirmed." [5]

The expected and usual commentary by the opponents of infant baptism upon these facts, would be that this unhappy situation is directly traceable to the unacceptable practice. They would agree with Rauschenbusch's opinion that "there was widespread doubt about infant baptism at the beginning of the Reformation, but to reject it would have meant churches of baptized believers and would have unchurched the great mass of men. The reformers recoiled from so sweeping a change, largely for political reasons, and infant baptism was maintained, defended, and extolled. It was an alien element in Protestantism, and has been most subtly influential in opening the door to other alien elements in worship, organization, and doctrine." [6]

There is no guarantee that infant baptism is the real culprit which causes this undesirable state of affairs. Although some would pinpoint Craig's sentence, "Baptism is something which has happened to them but not of their own seeking," as the most telling explanation of the matter, another sentence may be more enlightening: "Their lives correspond in no way to what is said about the nature of the Church" more appropriately underscores our major premise that paedobaptist churches have played false to their own baptismal doctrines and practices. These lives do not correspond because they have no correspondents in their churches. Gone is the solidarity of

[4] Clarence Tucker Craig, *The One Church* (Nashville, Tenn.: Abingdon-Cokesbury Press, 1951), p. 80.

[5] Winthrop Hudson (ed.), *Baptist Concepts of the Church*, chap. 3, "John Gill's Doctrine of the Church," by John W. Brush (Valley Forge, Pa.: Judson Press, 1959), p. 66.

[6] Sydnor L. Stealey (ed.), *A Baptist Treasury* (New York: Thomas Y. Crowell Company, 1958), chap. 4, "Distinctive Baptist Principles," "Why I Am a Baptist," by Walter Rauschenbusch, pp. 178-179.

the Christian family in terms of a former Judaeo-Christian structure. An infant baptized in these communions will be fortunate indeed if he is nurtured by either or both the congregation and the family which brought him to baptism. He looks in vain around him for the sponsoring, protective, nurturing community of faith. As he approaches, over the years, the event of confirmation, he finds the priests or ministers of his church pleading frantically with the members of the congregation not to expend their energies and talents in his behalf, but rather to look to their own salvation. Whatever one may think negatively of infant baptism, it is not a rite calculated in itself to reduce the membership rolls of the churches nor to make for a nominal membership. Instead, infant baptism is an exacting and demanding rite for the congregation in terms of its faith and practice.

What actually happens is the failure of the churches to be what they have promised. The congregation, which declares for infant baptism as an act of its own faith, does not prove to be faithful. The baptized infant is set adrift, bereft of a supporting faith.

Churches practicing believers' baptism reveal a different, but nonetheless serious, deviation. Most of these churches stem from sectarian origins. Baptism, as we have seen, devolved, in faith and practice, out of the sects' understandable emphasis upon spiritual experience as the qualifying factor by which one proved his right to membership in the true Church. If these churches are to remain true to their doctrine of believers' baptism—namely, prior faith and experience with the risen Lord and His Spirit and baptism as a following sign of that conversion—then a causal connection between profession of faith and Spirit visitation must be manifestly maintained.

The improbability of continuing as a sect in the present stage of religious sophistication complicates the sectarian position. On the one hand, the world mission enterprise militates against the wishful endeavor to avoid overorganized churches as a means to giving free access and movement to the Spirit within them. Despite the "local autonomy" of their individual churches, Baptists, for example, are a well-organized and efficient religious machine, working throughout their far-flung missionary ministries. Along with similar groups, they can no longer be classified as a sect. On the other hand, an excessive display of religious emotionalism is unfashionable and in bad taste so far as the larger Christian groups are concerned. Spirit-energized professions of faith are losing favor. The mantle of authority has been taken away from emotional spirituality and given to less colorful substitutes.

Groups and churches that continue to emphasize the sectarian quality of their faith ostensibly call attention to the manifestation of the Spirit at the time of conversion. But even these groups may maintain their enthusiasm by developing a "spirit" that is often disguised as the Holy Spirit. This is the spirit of being the group with the truth. It becomes a gathering largely nourished upon the feeling of being different from both the world and the other Christian organizations. Not infrequently, these groups develop an extreme moralistic religion that derives its spirit from animosity and hostility toward those who, in their judgment, are unrighteous and doctrinally false.

Another substitute spirit is that of congeniality. Sectarian groups are usually clannish in their inner loyalties as they withdraw from society at large. This "club mentality" is not confined only to the more extreme sectarian groups. It proves to be contagious among all middle-class churches. It is nevertheless more open and definable as it appears within the religious habits of the sectarian fringe.

One day while driving on a mountain road near the city of Charleston, West Virginia, I casually noticed, at an extremely sharp curve in the road, a sign familiar in that area. PREPARE TO MEET THY GOD, it shouted, above the screaming tires of the impious and indifferent, lest they hurl themselves into oblivion before "getting right."

Upon arriving in the city, the first church in view called out a cheerful welcome from its bulletin board: WELCOME, COME AND MEET YOUR NEIGHBOR. Meet God on a dangerous curve and your neighbor at church? Perhaps.

One of the greatest threats to sectarian religion is privilege. Sects find that they lose their children if the children receive a broad education and secure vested interests in society. Hence the sect fears middle-class respectability. There are exceptions to this rule among those who could be middle class but rebel against its supposed smug provincialism. Baptists and Disciples are prime examples of former sectarian groups which, having achieved a higher social status, are moving rapidly to church-type religious organizations.

Abhorring excessive emotionalism and holding more tolerant attitudes toward other Christians, these churches find it difficult to whip up a spirit of emotional hostility as a substitute for the Holy Spirit. In the interim they have discovered the spirit of activism. It is the business of each member to feel "team spirit" so as to keep the religious organization busy and efficient at its task. All too often such churches are characterized by an artificial enthusiasm which blends the tone of the carnival barker with the methods of the efficient advertising expert. Multiple activities for children, countless challenges for the time and energy of the young people, and committees ad infinitum for the adults keep up the spirit. The Spirit of the Risen Lord and the corresponding event of the resurrection are no longer necessary. But the churches are far from dead. There is committee work, young people's activities, religious car pools, little girls being baked into "Brownies," "mother bears" prolonging the estrangement between "Cubs" and "father bears," and prismatic little "Sunbeams" lighting up for Jesus.

Infant baptism is defunct for want of a sponsor. Believers' baptism, bereft of the Spirit, has spawned some incomprehensible substitutes. The infant is often baptized into a great doctrine which has no believers. The believer is baptized into a group of people too busy to take time to believe anything.

4 Evangelism

A connection between evangelism and baptism persists despite the efforts, mostly not deliberate, to drive a wedge between them. These divisive factors have nevertheless taken their toll, to the detriment of both baptism and evangelism.

Evangelism and infant baptism, although connected in form, are doctrinally irreconcilable. A pivotal example of this fact is provided by the ministry of John Wesley and his consequent influence upon the Methodist Church. Wesley was pushed to retain the practice of infant baptism because he did not wish to forsake completely his Anglican origin. His sharpest doctrinal conflict stemmed from his evangelistic endeavors, which brought inevitable questions to bear upon the paedobaptist position. Until this day, the Methodist Church reflects its founder's confusion in this respect. The ceremony for the infant is variously described—as dedication by the parents to rear their child in an environment of Christian nurture; as dedication of the infant, himself, to God and the Church; as baptism that awaits profession of faith or confirmation; or as baptism that is all sufficient, precluding the necessity of any succeeding ceremony. Having undergone some sort of infant rite, Methodists may consequently expect to renew the vows given at their baptism in order to join the church, or may be asked to make a profession of faith to qualify for membership—sometimes with baptism to follow—or their infant baptism may suffice as the only requirement for belonging to the "body of Christ," but not simultaneously afford them membership in the church.

Such a variety may have been spawned by one of Wesley's explanatory statements, namely, "Baptism is not the new birth; they are not one and the same thing. . . . From the preceding reflections we may . . . observe that as the new birth is not the same thing with baptism, so it does not always accompany baptism; they do not constantly go together. A man may possibly be 'born of water' and yet not be 'born of the Spirit.' There may sometimes be the outward sign, where there is not the inward grace." [7]

The motive for Wesley's argument here is evidently his suspicion of baptismal regeneration. Entrenched as he was in the supposition that one could grow into sanctification or perfection and receive a "second blessing," he cast doubt upon baptism being inextricably linked with being "born of the Spirit." This position forced him to a strange dichotomy. Baptism of a person old enough to be a believer and to receive the Spirit by conscious surrender was not efficacious. The simultaneous occurrence of "spirit-baptism" and

[7] Robert W. Butner and Robert E. Chiles, *A Compend of Wesley's Theology* (Nashville, Tenn.: Abingdon Press, 1954), pp. 268 f.

"water-baptism" was not assured. The connection would depend upon the faith of the believer.

Wesley's paedobaptist affinity pressed him to make an exception for infant baptism. In this regard he countered the first idea by explaining: "I do not now speak with regard to infants: it is certain our Church supposes that all who are baptized in their infancy are at the same time born again; and it is allowed that the whole Office for the Baptism of Infants proceeds upon this supposition." [8]

With the "supposition" that those baptized in infancy are born again confronting him, and with his desire for public and deliberate professions of faith on the part of the mature person as a means to renewal and spirit possession, Wesley's solution presented Baptists and Methodists particularly, as well as other groups, with one of their most persistent and divisive arguments. Those who come from these traditions may remember the heated debates between their fathers over the issues of "once in grace, always in grace" and "falling from grace," or "backsliding." Moreover, they discover, with unwarranted surprise, that this conflict still exists between these two Christian bodies, although it is refined by the use of modern theological terms.

Carrying his evangelistic endeavors to a congregation, most of which had been baptized in infancy, Wesley had to make allowances for a "fall from grace" on the part of those already baptized. Without this theological assumption, his endeavors at evangelism would have been unfruitful. The over-all result of his theology of baptism and evangelism reveals a twofold doctrine of baptism. Infant baptism was into salvation because it insured regeneration, new birth, and the gift of the Spirit. Baptism for adults was more like the baptism of John. It was then, and is now, essentially a baptism of repentance. A decisive commentary upon the foregoing premise explains that

it was from his religious experience under the influence of the Moravians that John Wesley got his message, but it was at the

[8] *Ibid.*, pp. 268 f.

corruption of England in the first half of the eighteenth century that the message was aimed. . . . The message was not centered upon God and man's rebellion against him, but upon man and his depravity and corruption and his inability to be moral without God's saving help through Christ. It was in this emphasis distinctly Pauline as compared even with Luther, because it was ethical in its emphasis and because it stressed the transformation of the nature of the individual. Wesley was "more concerned in escape from sin and the attainment of holiness than in escape from divine wrath and the attainment of peace with God!" The emphasis was upon regeneration and sanctification rather than reconciliation.[9]

This paradoxical treatment of baptism is fully revealed in the Book of Worship for the Methodist Church. A study of the orders for the baptism of infants, children and youths, and adults discloses that a distinction is made between each category with regard to the meaning and extent of sin and the relevance of baptism to such matters.

The mention of sin is absent from the order for the baptism of infants. The minister addresses the parents or sponsors as follows:

Dearly beloved, forasmuch as this child is now presented by you for Christian Baptism, and is thus consecrated to God and to his Church, it is your part and duty to see that he be taught, as soon as he shall be able to learn, the meaning and purpose of this holy Sacrament; that he be instructed in the principles of our holy faith and the nature of the Christian life; that he shall be trained to give reverent and regular attendance upon the public and private worship of God and the teaching of the Holy Scripture; and that in every way, by precept and example you shall seek to lead him into the love of God and the service of our Lord Jesus Christ.[10]

---

[9] Harrison Elliott, *Can Religious Education Be Christian?* (New York: The Macmillan Co., 1953), p. 163.

[10] *The Book of Worship for Church and Home* (Richmond, Va.: The Methodist Publishing House, 1945), pp. 390-391.

If these subjects are received into the Methodist Church while they are still children or young people, either or both their parents and sponsors are asked to renew the vows which they made when the children were first baptized.[11] After charging the parents, the infant is baptized by the name which his parents have given to him.

At the baptism of children and youths a different meaning is uncovered. There is apparently a partial, but not complete, responsibility laid upon them at their baptism. "Will you faithfully put away from you every known sin, of thought, word, or deed, and accept and confess Jesus Christ as your Saviour and Lord?" is the nature of the charge.[12]

The baptism of adults calls for a more open and direct act of repentance. A part of the order for the baptism of adults reads:

"Dearly beloved, who have come hither desiring to receive holy Baptism, the congregation gives thanks to God for your coming, and prays that the Holy Spirit may dwell within you, and that your faith may not fail. In the hearing of this congregation you should now make known your purpose to accept the obligations of this holy Sacrament.

"Do you truly repent of your sins and accept and confess Jesus Christ as your Saviour and Lord?" [13]

The Book of Worship of The Methodist Church seems to have been appreciably influenced by Wesley's theology on baptism and evangelism. As Elliott contends about Wesley's main interest, *The Book of Worship* moves from concern for the infant's reconciled relationship with God to involving the adult in the good life of sanctification, making certain that he vows to repent of his sins. The baptism of infants must have caused Wesley many anxious periods of doubt. It could not have been otherwise in the face of his evangelistic fervor. The candor of Leslie Church prompts him to say the only thing that can be said: "It is probably true to say that John Wesley was more vague in his teaching on Baptism, especially infant baptism, than on any other subject." [14]

[11] *Ibid.*, p. 405.
[12] *Ibid.*, p. 394.
[13] *Ibid.*, p. 397.
[14] Leslie Church, *More About Early Methodist People* (London: The Epworth Press, 1949), p. 250.

While Wesley was vague and sparse in his teaching about baptism, Luther was contradictory and prolific. He left the churchmen who bear his name no less confused than the Methodists.

The Director of Home Missions for the Evangelical Lutheran Church, Oscar Anderson, cites the fact that, within his church, an "inverse ratio" of evangelistic concern follows any noticeable appreciation for baptism. He notes the suspicion within the churches that "an emphasis on baptism and an emphasis on conversion cannot get along together." [15]

Turning to Luther for help, he continues:

> Luther would be heard speaking to some Lutherans who dismiss the efficacy of baptism in later life for the unbelieving adult when he scores the "dangerous error" which imagines that through sin "the strength of Baptism was destroyed and the ship had become leaky. Baptism remains a strong indestructible ship that is never broken apart into separate planks." He admits, "Certainly many frivolously jump out of the ship into the ocean and are brought to naught; those are they who fall away from the faith in the promise and plunge themselves into sin." "But," he adds, "the ship itself remains and continues its journey unharmed so that he who through grace can return to the ship is not conveyed to life on a plank, but upon the ship itself." [16]

Almost with a chuckle, one may imagine what the die-hard immersionist does with this metaphor. What Luther envisions as the plunge from the stout ship of baptism into the sinful water can suggest only real baptism to one who believes that much water is necessary. Lutheran evangelism, according to the Home Mission Director, is a two-directional endeavor. One way is toward conversion and a personal faith. The other is a return to conversion and personal faith. To use Luther's analogy, if one does not fall from the ship he is evangelized toward faith in the light of the promise of

[15] Oscar Anderson, *Baptism and Its Relation to Lutheran Evangelism* (Minneapolis, Minn.: Ausburg Publishing House, 1955), pp. 14 f.
[16] *Ibid.*, p. 12.

his baptism. If he falls from the ship, he is brought back to the faith. It does not occur to the proponents of this evangelistic scheme that one who never leaves the ship is directed toward personal faith which is not yet secured. The one who departs is to be brought back to a faith, which he must have received when he went overboard, since, if he does not take the plunge, he is still being evangelized toward faith. "Lutheran evangelism," Anderson explains, faces the baptized kept and the baptized fallen. In every congregation, Lutheran evangelism sees the elder son who remained in the Father's house, and the prodigal son who left the Father's house. And with the same message of repentance and faith it seeks to bring the former to acknowledge humbly his place in the home and the other to see his lost condition to lead him home again.[17]

For the sake of argument, let us take the liberty of imagining both sons transported from the father's house to Luther's ship of baptism. We may thereby understand the feast of the fatted calf. By leaving, the prodigal son achieved a faith to which he was now returning. By staying home, the elder brother was yet being evangelized toward eventual faith and conversion. His feast awaited the achievement of this goal. In short, he would have been better off had he also left home or jumped overboard.

One of the most notorious examples of the conflict between evangelism and infant baptism occurred in this country in the middle of the seventeenth century. It was a curious doctrinal compromise, called the Halfway Covenant. Two contributing factors should first be brought into focus. One factor hinged on Calvin's teaching that infant baptism was admission into the visible church. We should recall that, according to Calvin, the infant was already in the body of the Church before he was born, if he were the offspring of Christian parents. Baptism was preceded by the gift of adoption. Adoption was into whole and complete salvation, and baptism was its ratification. The logical outcome of this faith was the doctrine of a visible and invisible church. The infant, born of believing parents, was admitted to the visible church by baptism because he was already in the invisible church by election.

[17] *Ibid.*, pp. 13-14.

The second contributing factor to the introduction of the Halfway Covenant was revivalism, consonant with the Great Awakening. "The fact which is not generally realized," as Schenck sees it, "is that the practices of revivalism had an effect within the Presbyterian Church which in many respects was similar to that which Bushnell had to combat in the Congregational churches. This effect was manifested partly in a neglect of infant baptism, partly in emptying it of meaning in the life of a great many people, partly in aberrations or deviations in the doctrine of the Presbyterian Church as expressed in the Calvinism of the Westminster Standards. . . ." [18]

Revivalistic influences caused increasing emphasis upon saving faith and regeneration by the Holy Spirit among the churches of New England, including Congregational and Presbyterian. Although one had been baptized in infancy, he was not entitled to communion unless he could give acceptable and credible evidence that he had experienced salvation and the regenerative gift of the Holy Spirit. In turn, only those children who had at least one parent enjoying the privileges of full communion were eligible for infant baptism. If and when such children were given baptism, they were later required to make their personal profession of faith before they could partake of the Supper.

"The result of these arrangements," one historian observes,

was that within a few years the great mass of the population were deprived of full communion and so of citizenship and of the right to have their children baptized. It began to be asked by many, "What is the use of infant baptism, seeing that it confers no special privilege, civil or religious, apart from the personal profession of the person baptized? Why not postpone baptism until after the personal profession?" The discontent of the majority of the population at being taxed for the support of public worship and yet denied the privileges of membership for themselves and their families, and especially at being civilly dis-

[18] Lewis Bevens Schenck, *The Presbyterian Doctrine of Children in the Covenant* (New Haven, Conn.: Yale University Press, 1940), p. 2.

franchised, had become so general and demonstrative by 1657 that it could no longer be safely ignored.[19]

The Halfway Covenant was the measure adopted to satisfy the discontents. Parents who were willing to acknowledge God's claim in their lives and who would accept the discipline of the Church were permitted to have their children or infants baptized without a profession of faith on the part of the parents.

The status of the children baptized under these conditions presented a stubborn complication. It gave birth to a multiplicity of contradictory endeavors toward plausible solutions. One extreme result was described by Schenck as follows:

> It is clearer than day that many who are inwardly, or in respect of inward covenant, the children of the devil, are outwardly, or in respect of the outward covenant, the children of God. Hence, therefore, it is that when we say that children are in the covenant, and so church members, the meaning is, not that they are always in inward covenant and inward church members, who enjoy the inward and saving benefits of the covenant, but that they are in external and outward covenant, and therefore outwardly church members, to whom belong some outward privileges for their "inward and eternal good." [20]

Among the many articles which appeared in the wake of the decision for the Halfway Covenant was one by Solomon Stoddard entitled: "The Inexcusableness of Neglecting the Worship of God Under a Pretense of Being in an Unconverted Condition." Stoddard proposed that "they [the unregenerate] should be urged to come to the sacrament of the Lord's Supper as a converting ordinance." [21]

The case is clear-cut in this instance. Congregationalists and Pres-

---

[19] A. H. Newman, *Baptists.* Vol. II of the American Church History Series (New York: The Christian Literature Co., 1894), p. 183.
[20] Schenck, *op. cit.,* p. 55.
[21] *Ibid.,* p. 55.

byterians had capitulated, under the impact of rampant evangelism, to the Anabaptist view of the Church. The Church was composed only of regenerate believers. Believers' baptism was thereby strongly indicated. The refusal to act on the basis of their belief was evasion. Having robbed infant baptism of the great doctrines of prevenient grace and objective salvation, they made a shameful mockery out of the rite by insisting that it remain the form of baptism in their churches.

No doubt they were influenced by the realization that "the memory of clergy who refused burial in any form to unbaptized infants, or to those baptized by laymen . . . lies behind a great deal of obstinate anti-clericalism in English towns and villages. It also accounts for something more positive, the persistence of grandmothers in avoiding such embarrassment by insisting that the baby must be 'done.' " [22]

J. A. Quarles, writing for the *Southern Presbyterial Review* in those days of revivalism, was a more honest and courageous voice, albeit a rare one, among his contemporaries. Of infant baptism, he said, "This is the Lord's chosen way to perpetuate and extend his Church. It is the growth from within, like the mustard seed. . . . The regular, normal mode of increase is through the multiplication of Christian families, the blessings descending from generation to generation in an ever-growing ratio." [23]

Our American churches that practice infant baptism have refused to be counseled by the history of their own faith. They continue to want the evident advantages of paedobaptism. At the same time they envy the apparent success of those churches which are their opposite in the baptismal category. It is true that the churches practicing believers' baptism, accenting the profession of faith, personal experience of the Spirit, and a conscious decision for Jesus Christ appear to be more vital and active than those institutions of the previously mentioned category. This brings us to a consideration of evangelism in the life of the churches that practice believers' bap-

[22] George Every, *The Baptismal Sacrifice* (London: S.C.M. Press, 1959), p. 97.
[23] Schenck, *op. cit.*, pp. 150-151.

tism. When the facts are disclosed, paedobaptists may thankfully re-
linquish their envy.

Evangelism and believers' baptism have more in common than is
the case with evangelism and infant baptism. The corruption of
believers' baptism within and proceeding from an evangelistic setting is then all the more tragic—inexcusably so.

Charles Clayton Morrison's disinterest in baptism has been cited.
He wrote on the question in the interest of his ecumenical goals. It
is regrettable that he felt so pressured. Belonging to a tradition which
claims that regenerate membership is the only valid kind for the
Church, and thereby insists upon believers' baptism, Morrison's reductionism of the rite is persistent and appalling.

> Democratic as it is, heterogeneous as is its composition, the
> Church needs some act by which it may register in its corporate
> mind and in the soul of each member the reality of this communal
> life. Each recruit must feel that he belongs, that he has rights and
> privileges in the spiritual community. He must be made to feel at
> home. This sense of fellowship, of actually being a part of the
> social entity, is created by formal initiation-baptism. The welcome
> of individual members does not suffice, although without it the
> formal initiation is hollow. There must be a corporate act, repre-
> sentatively performed, in which the social will of the group meets
> the will of the individual and confers upon him the new status.
> This is what every initiatory act does—in the state, in marriage, in
> lodge and guild. In the Church this act is sacramental and properly
> so, because the freemasonry into which it introduces one is re-
> ligious.[24]

Morrison's view of baptism may be put in one succinct sentence.
A man is saved and is then baptized into his religious club. He is
made to feel at home by the act of baptism. The welcome of individual members is important but not quite enough. Baptism is a
wet, lukewarm handshake!

[24] Charles Clayton Morrison, *The Meaning of Baptism* (Chicago: Disciples
Publication Society, 1914), pp. 83-84.

The tradition to which Morrison belongs is caught in a basic contradiction. It should be said parenthetically that this contradiction is
more apparent in American churches than in their European counterparts, although the latter are not immune by any means. The contradiction has arisen because an emphatic note has settled upon the
believer and his belief in baptism, alongside the evangelistic focus
upon winning children to Christ at an early age. It is hard to take
believers' baptism seriously in the wake of a given church's revival
campaign in which children at the age of nine, give or take, are
subjected to mass evangelism. It is still common practice for guest
evangelists to appear at the Sunday-school hour in the junior department, seeking all those who will "give their lives to Jesus." After
a brief presentation of the "gospel," a show of hands is called for.
Moments later, children may throng the aisles in answer to the "invitation," and are accepted as believers. The innate guilt that
churches which engage in this practice actually feel appears when
the confession of some straggling adults stirs the congregation with
a sense that this is the genuine thing and that children must be accepted in a manner similar to that stated in Calvin's doctrine of presumption.

Gaines Dobbins has taught in Southern Baptist seminaries for a
number of years, and his book on the evangelization of children
exemplifies the basic contradiction in the above practice. Although
the book deserves strong criticism, Dobbins must be given credit
for being one of the very few in his tradition to endeavor to make
a serious approach to the problem.

Dobbins is vulnerable to the same accusation frequently directed at
the paedobaptists, namely, the desire to baptize children, as the easiest
means by which to populate the Church. "Churches have erred at
two extremes," he begins.

At one extreme are those who would baptize the child in its
infancy, hoping that thus the child will somehow be regenerated
by the grace of God mediated through the faith of the parents or
god-parents; or, if not, that the child will thus be brought into
the fold of the church, whose influence, combined with that of

parents, will make unnecessary and even undesirable a personal commitment. At the other extreme are those who would let the child alone. They would bring no persuasion to bear upon him, perhaps letting him wander far away into sin, in the hope that when God's good time comes he will, by an act of prevenient grace, snatch the erring one as a brand from the burning. In between lies the better way to clear New Testament teaching. The child is to be led toward Christ, to Christ, and into Christ through a personal experience which is all the better if it comes early.[25]

The preference for the "early personal experience" of a little child can hardly accord with an emphasis upon the believer and his believing in the context of believers' baptism. It is clear that the younger the child, the less important and credible his belief. The author is on precarious ground when he suggests that the churches should try to snare the child at a time when he knows enough to say "yes" but not enough to say "no" to the invitation to become a Christian.

Dobbins proceeds with an illustration that proposes an improbable solution to this incontrovertible difficulty. It becomes evident in the process that the accent on believing is shifted to an accent on the personal and subjective element in salvation. He offers a hypothetical situation in which a comparatively young boy is persuaded that he should become a professing Christian. Bobby, the boy in question, wishes to discuss the decision with his parents. The Sunday-school teacher, who has been instrumental in leading Bobby to this juncture of faith, demurs and wonders if this is necessary. He reminds Bobby that the questions of his need for a Saviour, of whether Jesus will save him if he is trusting, of whether he should "turn from a life of sin" and give his "heart to Jesus for a life of service," and of whether he has the right to make this choice for himself, are all questions which he ought to be able to answer for himself. Apparently, it does not register that the teacher is quite involved with the boy he is advising to stand alone.

Then the teacher finally explains: "There remains one other

[25] Gaines Dobbins, *Winning the Children* (Nashville, Tenn.: Broadman Press, 1943), p. 27.

question. Do you need to consult your parents as to whether or not you should make your public statement at this time and ask for baptism into the membership of our church?"

With growing comprehension Bobby replies, "Yes, that's it. I see now that all the rest is up to me."

"Right," answers the teacher. "So why not do what nobody else can do for you, here and now? Then talk over with your parents and pastor the practical matter of church membership, for that is something that has to do with others as well as yourself." [26]

For the sake of a reader unfamiliar with the plight of children in the churches practicing believers' baptism, it should be admitted that this is an extreme example. Many teachers would show greater wisdom than this hypothetical one. At the same time, no one ought to suppose that the illustration is so atypical as to be disregarded completely. Nor can the fact be ignored that a highly respected professor, of the tradition being discussed, offers this hypothetical incident as an example of a recommended procedure.

As a recommended practice it basically deviates from the doctrine of believers' baptism. Attention is redirected from the believing person to one in isolation. In other words, there is no New Testament indication that the act of belief is dependent upon isolation. A believer, so far as the New Testament is concerned, may, and usually does, come to belief in a community of faith. The mature person, seeking to discuss his dawning faith with others in the believing community, would not likely be shut off from his friends, certainly not from his parents, in the same kind of situation. The child is turned away from such resources in order to give the impression that he has not been unduly influenced by older and stronger minds. In endeavoring to make a believer of the young child, the churches make him a hermit. He is the victim of the grossest form of subjectivism. Little wonder that a junior high-school teacher heard one of her students report one morning: "Well, you'd never guess what I did last night. I went to the meeting and got myself saved."

The rabid desire for growth of church membership has made children the innocent parties to a subterfuge which tries simultane-

[26] *Ibid.*, pp. 43-44.

ously to hold up the façade of believers' baptism. Churches, unwilling to risk the chance of a mature person's negative reaction, plot their evangelistic schemes to win primary-school and secondary-school children to Jesus Christ. The only way to prove that the child is a "believer" is to disallow what may be outside influence. The child should be kept away from the influence of his parents in his endeavor to arrive at the Christian decision. At the moment of decision he is to stand alone, unable to share his wonder at the redemptive love of Christ with his parents and other members of his family. This is not only heresy but a remarkably cruel heresy. It undermines the fundamental Old Testament doctrine of the solidarity of the family. It makes a mockery of the witness of a believing community.

Numerous Baptist ministers have heard the glad but incomprehensible comment of parents who boast, "We are confident that our child knew what he was doing when he made a decision for Christ, because we had nothing whatsoever to do with it." Too few Baptist ministers retort, "May God have mercy upon you."

Dobbins' disposition of baptism is both predictable and disappointing. The significance of the rite is relegated to the practical matter of church membership. Since this has something to do with others, as well as the individual, it is an item about which no objection to discussion should be raised. Because baptism connotes congregational and community responsibility, Dobbins, following the custom of the frontier element, is careful to keep it separate from the profession of faith.

"The question of the child's public commitment and reception into church membership," he admits with seeming reluctance, "must usually be dealt with as a part of the procedure of winning him to Christ. It is important to keep the two matters separate, so far as the saving experience is concerned, but to bring them together at the point of duty. Obviously there is a time lapse between conversion and baptism, for the latter is conditioned on the former in the New Testament concept of faith salvation." [27]

Dobbins puts himself with others, before him, who aver that both baptism and church membership are appendages, albeit good ones,

[27] *Ibid.*, pp. 44-45.

to becoming or being a Christian, or both. In this regard, he says that "the child's choice of Christ having been made, the problem of church membership arises. Shall baptism and admission into full privileges and duties of church membership follow immediately? Practical wisdom and spiritual insight are demanded at this point. The child's tendency is to confuse his experience of salvation with 'joining the church.' The distinction should be made crystal clear. A church is an organized body of baptized believers who have joined themselves together on the basis of common experiences, common beliefs, common purposes. This they do because they are Christians and not in order to become Christians." [28]

As has been indicated, Dobbins is among the very few who have endeavored to write seriously about the evangelism of children in the believers' baptism community. This has made it necessary—regrettably so—to deal critically and at length with his book. It is possible to redress this admitted imbalance by contending, without fear of widespread contradiction, that the work is representative of the practices and doctrines of the churches with which he is concerned. What has been said about his treatment may be applied to the problem in general. In endeavoring to structure child evangelism, which is the next thing to infant evangelism, and uphold the doctrine of believers' baptism, Dobbins has succeeded in making one thing clear: Child evangelism and believers' baptism are not easily reconciled. His attempt at keeping child evangelism and believers' baptism inviolate moved him to isolate the child from his parents and the Church, as well as to remove baptism and church membership from a significant place in the Christian life. The Church is also reduced to a body of baptized believers who organize themselves because they have several things in common. The Holy Spirit is accorded no recognized human medium through which to approach the child and bring him to Christ.

Although considerable attention has been given to the problem of believers' baptism and child evangelism, this is by no means the only difficult problem to be faced. Mention of the Holy Spirit serves to remind us that the doctrine of the Spirit receives a hard buffeting

---

[28] *Ibid.*, pp. 120-121.

at the hands of the advocates of believers' baptism. In the preceding chapters the problem has been dealt with in its historical setting. The effect of the supposed discontinuity between believers' baptism and the gift of the Spirit upon evangelism is now of specific concern.

Believers' baptism cannot have the same relationship with the visitation of the Spirit as does infant baptism in Roman Catholic and Anglican communions. Henry P. Van Dusen's observation under- scores the difference: "It was left to the despised Anabaptists to claim that the inward voice of the Holy Spirit takes precedence over the external word of scripture or the dicta of the prelate. As in earlier periods, the claim was employed to justify all manner of ideas and behavior which outraged the theologians and scandalized the ecclesiasts. But also, once again the Holy Spirit was emancipated from the leading strings of dogma and the dead-hand of tradition to resume its guidance of the minds and hearts of the devout into new truth." [29]

The Anabaptist position concerning the Holy Spirit in this respect is generally consonant with that of Baptists, Disciples, and sects which have something in common with these larger denominations. Van Dusen proves to be an ally of the doctrine by contending that "ac- tually, the spirit comes most characteristically to individuals often when outside the immediate fellowship of the Church, and sometimes with directives defiant of the convictions and instructions of the Church. . . . The Holy Spirit is the principle of personal religious experience, of individual inspiration as such, it is the never-exhausted discloser of new truth." [30]

Without explicitly saying so, Van Dusen must surely have been talking about two situations instead of one, in the foregoing quota- tions on the Spirit. Let us discuss the latter point first. His declara- tion that the Spirit cannot be imprisoned by the Church to the ex- tent that no "new truth" is possible to a person who is not in "im- mediate fellowship" with the Church needs clarification. In such instances, when truth is needed, it may come by the Holy Spirit to

[29] Henry P. Van Dusen, *Spirit, Son, and Father* (New York: Charles Scribner's Sons, 1958), p. 82.
[30] *Ibid.*, pp. 58-59.

the individual in terms which defy the convictions and instructions of the Church. It ought to be made clear that this is not an "anti-Church" agreement between God and the individual. On the contrary, the work of the Spirit in this situation is for the sake of the Church as well as the individual. The person is not at the mercy of the Church's failure, so long as the Spirit may approach him even when he is not in "immediate fellowship." However, it is equally true that the Spirit leads the one whom it has chosen as a prophet to declare the word to the Church in order that the covenant community might be renewed. Any indication that the spirit-filled individual intends to keep his revelation—from the Spirit and his relation to the Spirit—from the Church, signifies that his connection with the Spirit is an abortive and ultimately ill-fated encounter.

In the instance of the "emancipation" of the Holy Spirit from the "leading strings of dogma and the dead-hand of tradition," the fact of salvation as a gift from God rather than a dispensation of the Church or of the Bible is made clear. Man need never depend upon church or written page for salvation. In the course of his redemption, however, the Spirit will not lead him to baptism only to release him to an act of initiation into the "body of Christ" from which the Spirit takes leave. In the case of the convert, the Spirit brings him to the Church through baptism, not by the coercion of the Church, but by the free volition of God. In short, the Spirit makes manifest to the Church and the world, in baptism, what has begun to take place in the individual. And the individual encounter can be no more than the beginning. If the person refuses the leadership of the Spirit which brings him to baptism, there will be no manifestation of the Spirit's visitation for the community of faith to behold. Nor is there any reliable evidence that the Spirit has ever chosen a symbolic substitute for manifesting its presence in the life of the individual.

Untold harm has been brought to the practice of believers' baptism by doctrinally disassociating it from the gift of the Spirit. It was improperly assumed, perhaps, that this was necessary in order to show that the encounter between the Spirit and the individual was not at the mercy of the Church or the Bible. To correct this erroneous assumption it must be recognized that one is brought to baptism by the work of the Spirit rather than by a directive from the Church or the Scripture. The free church, more than any other kind, having released, doctrinally speaking, the Spirit from Church and Bible, must offer some means of corporate expression. The most dramatic expression provided it by the Spirit is the believing community's incorporation of a new member through the act of believers' baptism. If and when it does not take place, there is every reason to believe that the Spirit is absent from the individual or the community, or both.

"The great event," Lampe proposes, "which changed Johannine into Christian Baptism was, as Von Baer, Cullmann, and Flemington have shown, the Baptism of Jesus, regarded first, as the Synoptists and the Fourth Gospel both imply, as the foreshadowing and symbolical summing up of His mission, as Son and Servant of God, of His death, resurrection, and ascension and of the New Covenant to be inaugurated in these events, and, secondly, as an event which prefigured and made possible the Pentecostal fulfilment of the ancient hope of a universal outpouring of the Spirit upon the people of God." [31]

Those who resent a proposed relation between baptism and the Holy Spirit should consider the available options. Mention has been made of the extreme manifestation of Spirit visitation by sectarian groups outside the main stream of Protestantism. We have talked about church enthusiasm as a substitute for the presence of the Spirit, either in the context of an exaggerated notion of close fellowship or by the activist complexes of the larger and more sophisticated churches. It is also revealing to look at the typical pulpit evangelism which occurs in this milieu.

Pulpit evangelism during a revival inadvertently discounts the relation between believing person and Holy Spirit by emphasizing the need of proper preparation for the coming of the Spirit. The successful revival depends upon four major musts: There must be the proper time, there must be the proper preacher, there must be the proper song leader, and there must be the proper soul-winning methods. The Spirit has no choice when confronted with these demanding

[31] G. H. W. Lampe, *The Seal of the Spirit* (New York: Longmans, Green & Co., Inc., 1951), p. 33.

preparations. He is commandeered in order that these earnest people may have a great revival. The Spirit does not come by His own calendar nor by being sent. He is pursued and prayed for until He is too exhausted to flee any longer. And if the Spirit cannot be trapped by the "mere preaching" of the gospel, an enterprising church may wish to secure the services of an evangelist, such as one who happily explained that his wife was a magician. "When the people grow tired of hearing the Gospel," he wrote, "Mary takes over with her magic."

A more devastating result in the long run is the pulpit evangelism which is practiced from Sunday to Sunday, week by week. More advanced churches are ready to do away with excessive and irrational emotionalism. Many of them are too large for a closely knit fellowship. They are also wearied with the excessive busyness of a programmatic church. These churches are generally impervious to the fact of the Holy Spirit, much less the work of the Holy Spirit. They tend to substitute a new intellectualism for the gift of the Spirit to the believer. Throughout its history, believers' baptism has stood counter to infant baptism because an infant could not be held responsible for his decision. Such accountability was primarily ethical and moral in nature. The need for intellectual understanding was secondary. It was only perceptible in the light of the ethical quality of faith. This is slowly being changed so that intellectual understanding is primary and ethical accountability is given second place.

Ecclesiasticism displaced the Holy Spirit in the Roman Catholic Churches. Literalism did likewise in the churches of the Reformation. Now intellectualism threatens to do the same in the churches of radical protestantism that originated in the left wing of the Reformation movement. The pragmatic result is the willingness of churches to baptize and enroll those "who know what they are doing" in an intellectual sense. The major setting for this trend is in the southern United States. Baptist, Disciples, and Methodist churches once appealed for the most part to the common man. The lack of money, aristocratic background, and education fitted an individual for these churches. Within a changing environment and circumstances, these church bodies have moved away from their sectarian nature. The children of the elder members of the churches named above are now receiving college degrees, joining the country club, living in the suburban green belt, sending their children to dancing classes, and making good incomes. With middle-class culture invading their homes, they shy away from emotionalism and will not tolerate the moralism or literalism of the "bible-belt mentality." They are still nonsacramental and nonliturgical in their worship, with emphasis remaining upon the believer; consequently the nature of belief has lost ethical content and deals almost entirely with intellectual understanding.

This would be bad enough were the new intellectualism beamed primarily at the mature. Instead, there remains a program for the evangelism of children. Christian doctrine, therefore, must be of a kind as to be intellectually comprehended by children. The drive toward intellectual maturity, which these churches need in proper measure, is rerouted for the sake of their children. The theologically oriented preacher is constantly harassed because he is not understandable to juveniles in his congregation. Some clergymen have made the horrendous mistake of preaching a children's sermon before they turn their attention to the adults. Not only is this an error in itself, but the preacher is frequently dismayed because the adults enjoyed his sermon to the children more than the one he delivered to them. They relish the opportunity to say so. This is the worst kind of intellectualism, since it must operate on the lowest possible level. The trend may ultimately lead toward adult baptisms and children's sermons. The preaching of the gospel will then be determined by the mental capability of a child.

It should be evident by now that the greatest difficulty which evangelism brings to the faith and practice of believers' baptism lies with the desire of the churches to multiply and grow. So long as this desire is implemented, the sharper and more desirable elements of believers' baptism, such as ethical responsibility, a regenerate and serious church membership, and true intellectual comprehension, are threatened with extinction.

5   Christian Education

Paedobaptists generally seem more confident about their ministry
of Christian education than with that of evangelism. They have reason
to be. Infant baptism is irreconcilable with evangelism, but this does
not hold true for its relationship with Christian education. In the
context of infant baptism, a child is a tender plant, freed from dis-
ease at its very roots, growing in the sheltering nurture of the church
school to the day it achieves the fullness of righteousness.

Confirmation is the chief complication in the otherwise happy
picture. Dom Gregory Dix's contention that infant baptism is an
abnormality which finds its corrective in confirmation has been sufficiently dealt with. Acceptance of his theory provides for an evangelistic note in Christian education that uses confirmation as an act of
personal confession and experience of faith. It acquires the stature
of a sacrament in this frame of reference.

Among those most adamantly opposed to Dix is Lampe, to whom
confirmation is a secondary rite falling short of sacramental heights.
In pursuing his argument, Lampe says that ". . . it is sufficient for
us to note that the fact the Christian Baptism is a re-presentation of
the Baptism of Jesus implies that it is through Baptism in water, and
not through any other ceremony such as physical anointing, that
the believer enters into the possession of the Spirit which is imparted through his membership in Christ." [32]

He concedes that the early church fathers were guilty of a mistaken
idea about confirmation. This was so when they interpreted the
rite in much the same way as Dix contends is proper. That misunderstanding has now been corrected by subsequent insights. "The
second, and more successful, reform," he advises, "was the relating
of Confirmation to Infant Baptism in such a way as to make it the
means of supplying the response of faith which is required in baptism but cannot be made in the case of infants. The emphasis came
to be laid increasingly upon the catechetical rather than the sacramental aspect of confirmation, that is, upon the preparation of the

[32] *Ibid.*, p. 45.

candidate and upon his confirmation in his own person of the baptismal vows made on his behalf by the god-parents." [33]

If Dix and his followers are right, confirmation is a sacrament which necessarily completes the sacrament of infant baptism. Christian education moves the child in the direction of a personal confession of faith, without which the prior baptism is suspect. If Lampe and his colleagues are right, confirmation is the end result of a process of instruction by which the individual comes to understand and make his own the effects of his infant baptism and the vows made thereto on his behalf.

So far as the perspective of Christian education is concerned, the scales are tipped in favor of the latter view. No man has influenced those scales more successfully than Horace Bushnell. He stands as the founder of the modern techniques of Christian education, and few have refuted him with any degree of success.

Bushnell, like Morrison, is not concerned with the subject of baptism in its own right. He has made baptism fit his theories on the religious education of children. His book on *Christian Nurture* does deal extensively with the subject of infant baptism, vigorously supporting the practice. At the same time, no man better serves to prove our major premise—that baptism has been appended to other doctrines with whatever modifications seem advisable—than does Horace Bushnell. Bushnell explains: "I have been thus full upon the rite of baptism, not because that is my subject but because the rite involves, in all its grounds and reasons, the same view of Christian education which I am seeking to establish." Subsequently, he argues potently on behalf of infant baptism by observing: ". . . it is my settled conviction that no man ever objected to infant baptism who had not at the bottom of his objections false views of Christian education." [34]

If Dix is to prevail in his argument about confirmation, he has to begin with the question of baptism and confirmation in their own

[33] *Ibid.,* p. 313.
[34] Horace Bushnell, *Christian Nurture* (New Haven, Conn.: Yale University Press, 1950), pp. 34-40.

setting. If the debate is allowed to start with the question of the
right kind of Christian education, Bushnell promises to have all the
better of it. His complete commitment to his view of Christian education is revealed not only in his attitude toward baptism as a
secondary consideration but by his same attitude toward the Lord's
Supper.

"I see no objection," he remarks concerning a baptized child,
"to his being taken to the supper casually, whenever his childish
piety really and seriously desires it; unless some opposing scruples
in the Church, or the minister, should make it unadvisable. Christ,
I am sure, would say—'Suffer the child and forbid him not.' " [35]

Those paedobaptists who endorse Bushnell most strongly have
not shown noticeable concern over what Bushnell's Christian education theory actually does to the sacrament of baptism. In the
final analysis, Bushnell renders infant baptism as unnecessary as
he makes believers' baptism undesirable. His concept of Christian
education is fathered by psychological rather than theological concern. Relatively speaking, whatever promises to be less traumatic and
disheartening to the child is endorsed. Over against the objectivity of
infant baptism as a theological reality, there is proposed a subjective psychological reality. Although the theology and psychology
of infant baptism appear to follow the same course, they follow it
with a different reason and for a different purpose. Theologically
speaking, the cause of objectivity is asserted. Psychologically speaking, subjectivity is accorded the dominant role.

Bushnell's classic definition reads: "What is the true idea of
Christian education? I answer in the following proposition, which
it will be the aim of my argument to establish, viz.: 'That the child
is to grow up as a Christian and never know himself as being otherwise.' " [36] It is common knowledge that the educator couches this
dictum in the assumptions he makes about the "organic unity of the
family." He comes close to Calvin's theological position that the child
should be baptized because he has been adopted by God before he
is delivered from the womb. The point of departure is not, however,

[35] *Ibid.,* p. 312.
[36] *Ibid.,* p. 351.

that of God's elective will and decisive act. His point of departure is that God has so structured the family that the child should be baptized because of the organic unity of his household. The child is not purposefully influenced by the family in an environmental sense, but is organically determined by the family, and without the family's conscious intention or knowledge.

E. Y. Mullins was one of the few to tackle Bushnell's position with any vigor. The effectiveness of his disputation is open to question. He appeared to be on solid ground when he insisted that the distinction between the church and family must be maintained. Bushnell had come perilously close to insisting that by nature the child was a member of the church. Even infant baptism, by its very practice, does not jibe with this assertion. Unfortunately, Mullins did not proceed with this line of thought. He turned to the question of pedagogy and accused Bushnell of endorsing unsound teaching principles. Infant baptism was thought to be forced upon the child, causing him to bear a burden of understanding which his immaturity would not allow. This was to miss Bushnell's emphasis upon the child's relaxed and assured growth in Christian nurture, even while he is unconscious of the process. That sounds like anything but an imposition.[37]

Bushnell's theory of salvation, rather than his understanding of the method of Christian education, is more vulnerable to probing questioning. His insistence upon the organic unity of the family as the foundation for becoming and being a Christian is his major weakness. As has been suggested, his concern that the child be spared discouragement or any traumatic experience—like the discovery that he is not a Christian—prompts his scheme of thought.

This succeeds not only in disparaging infant baptism but confirmation as well. Speaking of the confirmation occasion, he advises: "Then, when they come forward to acknowledge their baptism, and assume the covenant in their own choice, they ought not to be received as converts from the world, as if they were heathens coming into the fold, but there should be a distinction preserved, such as

---

[37] E. Y. Mullins, *The Axioms of Religion* (Philadelphia: American Baptist Publication Society, 1908), chap. 10, "Christian Nurture."

makes due account of their previous qualified membership; a form
of assumption tendered in place of a confession—something answer-
ing to the Lutheran confirmation, passed without a bishop's hands." [38]

The person at confirmation is led to assume that he is a Christian
because he has never known the day when he was not. He confesses nothing, since he has never known anything to confess. Bushnell rules out the objective reality of sin. If at confirmation one did
more than acknowledge his baptism and also acknowledged sin,
which the paedobaptists believe infant baptism to have overcome,
then the child would know that he had been other than a Christian.
For Bushnell, the child is almost a Christian by thinking himself to
be. By confessing that infant baptism is his choice, because it involves the concept he holds for Christian education, it goes without
saying that he would dispense with the entire doctrine and practice
if it proved destructive to his theory. He does in fact dispense with
a part of the doctrine of infant baptism by making both sin and
regeneration something less than objective realities. The one thing
missing in Bushnell's pat procedure is a frame of reference in which
one may know oneself as a Christian. Never to know oneself as
"otherwise" is not to know oneself as he is. In this category of Christian education, the individual can neither refer to his baptism nor to
his confirmation as a means of knowing what he is. In making sure
that the child never knows himself to have been other than a
Christian, Bushnell inadvertently makes it more difficult for the
individual to have any assurance that he *is* a Christian. His protégés
would never notice the great light, for they are blind to the darkness.
Consciously they never pass from death unto life. Nor do they feel
the love of God for the sinner they never were. These great para-
doxes are never brought to the consciousness and conscience, either
by a profession of personal faith or by the prefigurement of infant
baptism which is later to become a reality in the life of the believer.

Despite the difficulty dependent upon confirmation, there is more
in common between infant baptism and Christian education than
there is between Christian education and the practice of believers'
baptism. There is as much difficulty reconciling the latter with

[38] Bushnell, *op. cit.*, p. 162.

Christian education as there is reconciling infant baptism with evangelism. No category of their ministry has been subjected to greater and more amazing distortion than has Christian education in the churches of believers' baptism. Under the guise of education, the church schools of these denominations are primarily engaged in the task of evangelism. For example, the 1962 Sunday School Convention for North Carolina Baptists met under the motto "Outreach for the Unreached." Typical of this inadvertent preoccupation with evangelism rather than basic education are two articles appearing in *The Young People's Teacher,* of the Southern Baptist Sunday School Series for the month of January, 1963. In an article entitled "Committed to Win," the author outlines a motif for winning lost people to Christ through the evangelistic medium of the Sunday-school class. It takes form with these steps: (a) "There are many reasons for attempting to win young people to Christ." (b) "The best place to begin to win young people is with a week-by-week effort to enroll lost young people in the class." (c) "Begin to cultivate those lost pupils who are being added to the class roll." Under the last topic appear these suggestions for winning an unbeliever: "First get to know him as a person. Second, get the pupil to be in the class sessions and in the worship services of the church as often as possible. Third, invite him to the socials and more informal gatherings of the class and church. Fourth, use the natural opportunities which come to talk to the pupil about his relationship to Christ. Fifth, when you feel that God is dealing with him, speak to him about your interest and your desire to help." [39]

There is not the remotest reference here to the content or method of Christian education. Nor was any intended. The writer is an associate professor of evangelism on the faculty of one of the Southern Baptist seminaries. It is a safe assumption that he wrote this article at the suggestion of the editors of the Sunday School Board. It becomes apparent, however, that the concept of the Sunday school's task in the mind of a professor of evangelism is little

[39] D. P. Brooks (ed.), *The Young People's Teacher* (Nashville, Tenn.: Sunday School Board of Southern Baptist Convention, 1962), "Committed to Win," by Kenneth Chafin, pp. 6-8.

different from that of those who write the curriculum. In a column under the by-line, "Your Editor Speaks," an article, "Our Imperative Task," drums out the call to evangelism: "One of the greatest forward steps in evangelism through the churches was taken when the Sunday School's possibility for outreach and witness was recognized. The development of a program of Bible study for persons of all ages presented the churches with an instrument of effective contact with the unsaved which would enlist them in group study and expose them to the convicting and converting influence of the Holy Spirit. Southern Baptists, particularly, have demonstrated the value of the Sunday School for reaching the lost and winning them to Christ and the church." [40]

Bible study merits token recognition from the above, but it clearly asserts that the chief imperative of the Sunday school is reaching the unsaved. Although leaving much to be desired so far as Christian education is concerned, these articles are forthright and realistic. They reflect, consciously or otherwise, the basic irreconcilability between Christian education and believers' baptism. The plight of young people and adults desiring Christian education through their churches is a despairing one. If they belong to those churches which practice infant baptism and confirmation, they find that adult classes in education are exceedingly hard to establish and maintain. Confirmation smacks too much of a graduation exercise. There is, after all, very little to teach a "confirmed Christian." He has little left to learn. In churches of the other variety, adult classes offer two substitutes for education: togetherness, and an opportunity to win the lost.

Without the twin assurances of infant baptism and confirmation, in the wake of which there may be no adult education whatsoever, the classes in adult education for these churches have little choice but to continue to evangelize the lost in their midst. If the teachers gear their lessons to the level of professing Christians, the unbeliever and the unchurched can be no more than a spectator. This is not

[40] D. P. Brooks (ed.), *The Young People's Teacher* (Nashville, Tenn.: Sunday School Board of Southern Baptist Convention, 1962), "Our Imperative Task," by Donald Ackland, p. 11.

only a discourtesy; it makes a mockery of the parable of the lost sheep. Consequently, the teacher preaches a sermonette to the "sinner," which the Christians usually enjoy more than the sermon, if they happen to remain for worship. And the "sinner" remains singularly untroubled throughout the sermon, since the fellowship of the class makes him feel right at home.

Christian education for children, especially those of the prebaptized age, constitutes a different problem. Bushnell's influence is continually cropping up in both method and content wherever Christian education for children is seriously undertaken. The height of irony is achieved by a church that defends believers' baptism with every possible resource, only to resort to the scheme of Bushnell for its program of education in the lower grades.

This trend is not overtly apparent. Seldom, if ever, does a church or clergyman in this category openly and deliberately embrace Bushnell's position. George Hill, an English Baptist clergyman at the beginning of the century, is a rare exception. Bushnell's caricature of Baptists who "tell the child that nothing but sin can be expected of him" prompted Hill's retort that such statements have no basis in fact and should not be allowed to stand.

"There is nothing in Baptist beliefs," Hill countered, "that may not be harmonized with the theory of Bushnell that children should be 'nurtured in the admonition of the Lord' from their earliest years, and be trained with the hope and expectation that they will grow up Christians from childhood, never knowing themselves as being otherwise." [41]

This attempted reconciliation between Bushnell and the Baptists fails to be convincing. For the most part, Hill begins and ends, as Bushnell did, with a psychological concern for the child's being spared the trauma indigenous to confession of sin and the surrender of one's life to the Saviour. A serious misunderstanding of baptism forms a part of his argument.

"In the light of this exposition it will be seen how easily and naturally the place of baptism in the religious life is determined.

[41] Thomas Stephens (ed.), *The Child and Religion* (New York: G. P. Putnam's Sons, 1905), "Baptists and Their Children," by George Hill, p. 293.

Baptism on its human side is the expression of a personal decision; on its divine side it is a symbol of spiritual regeneration; and so it is rightly administered when the decision has been made and the regeneration effected." [42]

Hill found it possible to agree with Bushnell by virtue of his casual attitude toward baptism. Ease and naturalness seduced Bushnell and brought about his passionate embrace of infant baptism. The realities of believers' baptism are not likely to be wooed by the same seductive qualities. These realities make themselves heard above the screams of selfish children, stridently demanding their own way, proclaiming that the will of God is supreme. They push like ugly excrescences through the contented surface of the child, presuming his natural innocence, with vivid reminders of latent sin. They interrupt the assumed continuity of his growth with demands for repentance—a reversal of his progress toward maturity—with the explicit judgment that he has been going the wrong way. They make it appear that the symbol of God's love is not a cradle but a cross. And thus the love of the Father becomes a judgment. It is not love drawn to them because of their magnetic winsomeness. It is love coming from sources which are not of their deserving.

Advocates of believers' baptism must realize that they contend for a conversion experience which is marked by confession of one's known and deliberate sin. No exception from this requirement ought to be granted to children. This poses an intrusive discontinuity in the life of the child unless he is taught from the first that he is a conscious and deliberate sinner, estranged from God by his own doing. Whatever price is demanded by this unpleasant prospect must be paid if believers' baptism is to be upheld. If it means that the rite has to be postponed until the individual is psychologically ready to withstand its impact, there is nothing to do but to accept the fact and abide by it.

One major denomination in the United States reveals a marked reluctance to pay this price. I speak of the Baptists. Because I belong to this company, I have chosen to make my point at our expense. The reader may be sure that a study of other groups, hold-

[42] *Ibid.*, pp. 305-306.

ing to the doctrine of believers' baptism, would produce the same results.

A brief statement on procedure is indicated. A number of department heads and lesson writers employed by the publishing media of the two major white Baptist conventions, American and Southern, were asked through correspondence whether they agreed with Bushnell's dictum: "A child should grow up as a Christian, never knowing himself to have been otherwise." Without exception the replies were in the negative; in most instances the need for a confession of conscious and deliberate sin was cited.

The next step was to go to the literature itself, much of which was written either directly by the correspondents or under their supervision. The results speak for themselves. Generally speaking, the material studied, while endeavoring to support the necessity of personal decision, tends to make the child feel an important part of the Church before he is a Christian. Simultaneously it would delay baptism and church membership after his profession, to make certain that his profession is valid, seek a smooth transition in the conversion experience, make baptism relatively unimportant, and avoid the realities of sin and death.

An example of the first objective is taken from a *Primary Superintendent's Manual*: "There are some real values and some serious problems connected with delaying church membership for children."

The problems should perhaps be listed first: (a) There is scriptural evidence that baptism always immediately followed conversion; (b) Baptism's purpose is to indicate a public profession. It is confusing to explain the purpose of baptism to a child who has made a public profession and then go on to say he must not yet be baptized; (c) Delay sometimes discourages a child and could even turn a child from the desire to make a commitment. On the other hand, some values may accompany such a delay: (a) A period of time between making public profession and being received for baptism may help a child understand that he is doing two separate things—giving himself to Jesus and joining the Church. [The contradiction between this and (b) in the preceding paragraph is noteworthy.] (b) Delaying church membership gives parents and pastors opportunity to make more certain that the child has given himself to Jesus and has made a valid commitment. Dealing with a child often takes several conferences over a period of time; (c) Often when there is little doubt of a child's trust in Jesus, there is evidence that he lacks the experience and understanding to make him a capable church member. [Church membership is after all more than being a believer—one regenerated by his trust in Christ; it demands experience and the ability to understand. Desertion of the principal theory of the nature of the Church is plain.] (d) Baptism and the Lord's Supper are symbolic ordinances most difficult for a child to understand; (e) People who favor delay feel that it cannot hurt the child who has had a real conversion experience. [Compare this with (c) in the preceding paragraph.] [43]

The possible value in delaying the child's membership in the Church having been granted, the literature reveals an assumed need for a compensating factor which may offset any ill effects accruing from postponement. As a consequence, the child is taught that he is a part of the Church and in fellowship with God, whether he is a Christian by profession or not.

". . . not all the children participate enough to feel part of the total church program. Many are unaware of the numerous ways in which all who attend church services and organizations work together to help others. They need to know more about the over-all work of the Church, even though neither they nor their parents are church members.

"Every child in the department can help the church do its work, and every child needs to feel that his share is important." [44]

In the same vein is literature appearing under the title, "Objectives for the Christian Education of Kindergarten Children." Referring to

[43] *Primary Superintendent's Manual* (Nashville, Tenn.: Southern Baptist Sunday School Board, 1961), Book 3, "Primaries and Church Membership," by Lavern Ashby, p. 44.

[44] *Eight Year Teacher* (Nashville, Tenn.: Southern Baptist Sunday School Board, 1961), Book 1, p. 130.

the child and the church, it advises: "Before a child is four he should come to think of his church as a special place where he feels at home, where families and good friends enjoy being together to worship and work and learn more about God and Jesus.

". . . We will lead him to love his church and increasingly to feel himself a loved and respected member of the church family, doing his part as he comes there to work, play, and worship with friends, and share with others through gifts and service." [45]

A similar emphasis is applied to the child's relationship to God. "The child's spiritual growth depends upon his growing relationship with God, expressed through love for God and confidence and faith in him. This is basic to an abundant Christian life.

"Through all his experiences with the world of nature and of persons we will try to lead the kindergarten child to feel a sense of fellowship with God who is still actively at work in his world." [46]

One is not disposed here to argue the merits of this educational approach to the small child. The important point is that these conceptual relationships between the child and the Church and between the child and God in no way correspond to what is taught in the doctrine of believers' baptism.

Bushnell's far-reaching influence is much in evidence in the above quotations. The insistence that the child needs to feel that he belongs has been one of his major emphases. That insistence shows up in strange places, not the least strange of which are these instructions to a teacher of eight-year-olds in Baptist environs.

The trauma which Bushnell wanted to avoid is compounded in this instance. If a child is made to feel at home in the church, both in the sense of belonging while not belonging, and of making an important contribution to the mission of the church by his participation, he is due for an abrupt and rude awakening when confronted with the necessity for conversion and church membership. Little wonder that children, in these instances, are incredulous, seeking some explanation for God's sudden departure from their once-secure lives.

[45] *Kindergarten Teacher's Book* (Philadelphia: Judson Press, 1955), Year 2, Winter, Part 2, p. 134.
[46] *Ibid.,* p. 133.

The churches requiring profession and believers' baptism for
church membership have cushioned the impact of the need for confession with a soft intellectual pillow. Children are unobtrusively conditioned to believe that they become Christians when they can answer
questions asked by a clergyman. A list of such questions, making
certain the child is "ready," is as follows:

(a) Ask him to tell you why he wants to join the Church; (b)
If he uses adult terminology, ask him to tell you what he thinks
he means; (c) Ask questions that he has not memorized the
answers for. Be sure the questions require more than a simple
"yes" or "no"; (d) Get the child to express how he feels in his own
words. Wait for him to do so. Refrain from putting words in his
mouth or from suggesting the answer you want; (e) Avoid using
theological phrases yourself. Use simple words, but be sure that
what you are saying is the simple truth; (f) If the atmosphere is
right, ask him to talk to God about the matter right then. You
can judge much from the type of prayer the child prays; (g) In
the conversation, watch for evidences that the child is conscious
that he has done things that make God unhappy, "a sense of
sin." [47]

If the child gets at least a "C" on this examination, it is presumed
that he is Christian and ready for church membership. Often the
would-be church member learns from an older sibling or close
friend, already graduated, the questions to expect before he takes the
test.

An attitude of reluctance to allow baptism a significant part in
the child's approach to a personal decision is manifested in the
same literature.

It is logical that the outward evidences of church membership,
baptism and the Lord's Supper, should first attract the attention

[47] *Primary Superintendent's Manual* (Nashville, Tenn.: Southern Baptist
Sunday School Board, 1961), Book 3, "Primaries and Church Membership,"
by Lavern Ashby, pp. 44-48.

of children. These visible concrete experiences are those on which the deeper experiences are based.

The usual reason for a child's questions is his natural curiosity. Many people feel that, when a child begins to ask questions about baptism and the Lord's Supper, he is ready for church member-ship. But to equate such questions with a readiness for church membership is as reasonable as to feel that a child is ready for marriage when he asks questions about a wedding he has at-tended.[48]

The sentence which suggests that baptism and the Lord's Supper are concrete experiences on which deeper experiences have their basis or foundation is certainly confusing. But the semantic problem must not distract us from a more serious dilemma. If baptism and communion have a basic connection—of whatever kind—with the deeper experiences of personal faith and commitment, it is illogical and self-defeating to presume that a child's questions about these events are irrelevant and demonstrate no more than his "natural curiosity." There is no room here for the Holy Spirit's intervening work which could, quite reasonably, prompt these questions on the part of the child.

The destruction of baptism continues:

Baptism is a symbolic ordinance given by Jesus as an initiation rite for those who become his followers and join the community of his followers. It symbolizes Christ's death, burial, and resurrec-tion and an individual Christian's death to sin and resurrection to new life.

The symbolism of baptism—that it represents death, burial, and resurrection—will be lost to the children. In helping children un-derstand the meaning of baptism, it might be wise to put em-phasis on the purpose: to show everyone you have given your-self to Jesus, and that from now on you want to do the things that please him.[49]

[48] *Ibid.*, p. 43.
[49] *Ibid.*, p. 48.

In the first of the foregoing paragraphs, the purpose of baptism is stated as being that of Christian initiation symbolizing identity with Christ in his death and resurrection. This purpose proceeds from Christ's gift of baptism to the Church and the individual. In the second paragraph—since the symbol seems hard for children to understand—the purpose is changed and it is stated that baptism is evidence that the child wants to "please Jesus," having given himself to Him. What Christ has given for Christian initiation, the churches use to make Jesus happy.

The realities implicit in believers' baptism are considerable, and demand confrontation. The desire to spare the child these realities is everywhere evident in the teaching of children by the churches concerned. A child confronting the reality of death will not always hear the gospel in answer to his question about it: "Talking about death may not come naturally . . . but it is well to be prepared for it. Help the children to think of death as an orderly part of God's plan. Children can begin to understand that our bodies are only houses in which we live, and that when we die we leave our bodies behind and live with God.[50]

When believers' baptism is taken seriously, it is difficult to see how this doctrine of death can be taught. The great theme of "bodily resurrection," not the resurrection of flesh and blood but the resurrection of the whole man, so vividly enacted in baptism, is here obscured by Greek mythology.

These examples have been offered only for the sake of pointing out the basic dilemma facing those who engage in Christian education of the prebaptized child. The attempt to circumvent the discontinuity in his religious growth brought to bear by the event of believers' baptism is productive of confusion and unconscious evasion. In most instances, when the endeavor is made, baptism is sacrificed as the first expendable. So long as believers' baptism remains in focus, the dilemma facing those who work for the Christian education of young children will persist until some other solution is achieved.

A distinguished educator, whose tradition is paedobaptist, offers

[50] *Kindergarten Teacher's Book* (Philadelphia: Judson Press, 1956), Year 2, p. 21.

an unmistakable challenge to all who are involved in the Christian education of children. Inadvertently, he judges those who would make the Christian pilgrimage an intellectual one and those who disparage the value of rich symbolism for children.

When a five-year-old asks, "Why did Jesus die?" the answer must be in terms of factual information within the grasp of the child, but it must also express the attitude of the teacher toward the child and communicate something of the Christian faith in the face of death. The teacher who can distinguish the difference between casual curiosity and the real theological predicament of the small child knows that the whole meaning of the Gospel is involved here, for the Gospel is God's answer to man's needs in the face of death in all its aspects. The new life of the Gospel, as symbolized by the resurrection, is relevant to the security and faith of the child.

Attempts to communicate the deeper meaning of the atonement and incarnation are thwarted by the inadequate vocabularies and concepts of this age. Jesus is either a superman or a God disguised as a man, either a prophet or someone who fooled the people by "seeming" to be a man. This problem needs to be faced although there is no clear-cut solution.

Most likely the answer may be suggested in the worshiping life of the congregation, for when children share the assumptions of a congregation that worships Jesus Christ as Lord and Saviour he finds him as their Redeemer in the preaching of the Word and the reception of the Lord's Supper, they intuit the relationship even when they cannot understand it. The child who worships with his parent and his teacher recognizes that they accept Jesus as Lord. The child who hears prayers addressed to God as Father, Son, and Holy Ghost and who sings, "Holy, Holy, Holy . . . God in Three Persons blessed Trinity," may not have an intellectual understanding of the mystery, but the Church's way of worship rubs off on him. Explanation does not help much, at this point, but example does.[51]

[51] Randolph Crump Miller, *Biblical Theology and Christian Education* (New York: Charles Scribner's Sons, 1956), pp. 97-99.

A child in the churches with which we have been dealing should
not be robbed of the advantage of the symbol of believers' baptism.
There can be no doubt but that this is what often transpires. The
curtain drops on the picture of life and death—the symbol is hushed
—all he hears is a preacher asking questions.

6 Worship

Worship is the occasion of God's self-revelation. God takes the
initiative. If He does not, man cannot worship Him. Not Presence
only, but revealed Presence, is necessary to worship. Otherwise, the
religious community invisibly reproduces the Athenian monstrosity
—an unseen statue to an "unknown God" because of His "unre-
vealed presence." This is modern man's dilemma and it commits
him to a two-sided idolatry. At the extreme of sacramentalism, God
is given substance by the sacramental act to the degree that He is
completely identified with it and is never separable from it. The
ultimate opposite polarity to this is the absolutely nonsacramental
process of identifying God with one's feelings about Him. The individual then worships his "worship" of God. The first extreme is
sacramental magic. The second is emotional magic. God is in neither.
He cannot be wholly subjectified by a sacramental act nor subjectified by an emotional lasso.

Sermon-centered congregations are often guilty of extreme subjectivism. The standard Sunday-school record used by the majority
of Southern Baptist churches, for example, has as one category in a
six-point system a section marked "preaching attendance." Worship is interpreted as the congregation's response to the sermon. The
congregation assumes that it has become focal and that it avoids a
"magic sacramentalism" by its own digestion of the word as a gathered priesthood of believers. Brunner's reminder has relevance in
regard to these churches:

> The Sacraments are the divinely-given flying buttresses which
> save the Church from collapse. In how many of the churches of
> today do we not find the Sacraments almost the sole biblical foot-
> ing—the only biblical element that has been able to withstand the

caprices of the gifted minister who lives by his own wisdom rather than from the Scriptures. Even the most audacious minister has not dared to lay hands on the Sacraments. And they are what they are! One may so interpret the words of Scripture that the words speak the opposite of their intent; but the Sacraments, thank God, speak a language independent of the language of the pastor. They are a part of the message of the Church least affected by theological or other tendencies; and that is their especial blessing.[52]

The question of objective worship versus subjective worship continues to perplex the Church. So long as the answer must be either/or, the confusion will linger on, diminishing the chance for remedy. Objectivists mistakenly assume that they have only to view God's self-knowledge and self-revealing as if His revelation is a drama to which they are interested spectators. The subjectivists make God the spectator and assume that He will know Himself as He sees their interpretative response to Him.

God must be worshiped in spirit. The objective reality of this fact issues from Paul's word to the Corinthians: "For the Spirit searches everything, even the depths of God. For what person knows a man's thoughts except the spirit of the man which is in him? So also no one comprehends the thoughts of God except the Spirit of God." [53]

"Paul does not develop this conception further," according to Hendry, for his interest is not in the fact that God knows himself, but in the fact that he shares that knowledge with others, by giving them his Spirit. The dominant thought is always of the Spirit as going out from God to others, as in the passage immediately following: "Now we have received not the spirit of the world, but the Spirit which is from God, that we might understand the gifts bestowed on us by God. And we impart this in words not taught by human wisdom but taught by the Spirit, interpreting spiritual truths to those who possess the Spirit." [54]

[52] Emil Brunner, *Our Faith,* trans. John W. Rilling (New York: Charles Scribner's Sons, 1936), pp. 127-128.
[53] I Cor. 2:10b-11.
[54] George Hendry, *The Holy Spirit in Christian Theology* (Philadelphia: The Westminster Press, 1956), p. 33.

God knows Himself by His Spirit and not by our interpretation and response. The worship of God depends upon the objective fact of His self-knowledge. But Hendry's fine interpretation also declares the subjective nature of worship because we are given the Spirit by which God knows himself and by which we also know Him: "The Spirit which is from God, or 'proceeds' from God, makes God known to us, because the Spirit is God's knowledge of Himself, and we can know God only as he shares his self-knowledge with us. But God does not make himself known to us by the immediate impartation of his Spirit; the gift of the Spirit is inseparably bound up with the mediation of Christ." [55] With these words, Hendry sounds the keynote of Christian worship. Man worships God in the Spirit which is mediated by Jesus Christ. Christian worship, therefore, is "Trinitarian worship" in the name of the Father, Son, and Holy Spirit. Here the implications of baptism for Christian worship are displayed. For, if there is one thing upon which the Church has agreed, it is that baptism is in the name of Father, Son, and Holy Spirit.

Hendry has still another helpful word concerning comprehending the meaning of worshiping God in Spirit. In John, chapter 4, Jesus declares to the woman of Samaria that God is spirit and must therefore be worshiped in Spirit and Truth. The common assumption has prevailed that Jesus pointed to God's universality. He was to be worshiped universally, and thereby the question of worship in Jerusalem or on Mount Gerizim was inconsequential. This is to forget that for John, as for Paul, spirit is contrasted to flesh, or the human realm, rather than matter or body, which is localized. The precise opposite to the concept that God is to be worshiped everywhere is intended. God is to be worshiped only in Spirit. Men cannot worship God unless they are given the Spirit by which to worship, and the Gospel declares that the Spirit has been given by the mediation of Christ. "God actively seeks men to worship him in spirit and truth by making himself accessible to them in his Son, who is the truth incarnate, and by the mission of the Spirit, who is the Spirit of truth." [56]

[55] *Ibid.*, p. 33.
[56] *Ibid.*, pp. 31-32.

Baptism is an act of worship. It both implies and is associated with the gift of the Spirit. In whatever denomination, the degree to which baptism is pushed aside will indicate the degree of profundity of the worshiping body. Karl Barth denounces the "strange gap in the baptismal teaching of all confessions—the Reformed included— that the meaning and work of baptism have never been understood in principle as a glorifying of God, that is, as a moment of His self-revelation. While baptism does its cognitive work, while the divine-human reality illuminates a man, making him an enlightened one, the far greater and primary thing occurs: God receives Glory in that He Himself, as man recognizes Him in truth, once more secures His just due on earth." [57]

Written in the early part of the present century, the following has an uncomfortably familiar sound:

> The Congregationalists do not believe in Baptism as much as the Baptists do. They are not as much in earnest about it. For Baptists, as for Catholics, the Church is the company of the baptized. But surely it should not be a reason for preferring infant Baptism that we need not spend so much interest on it. We neglect Baptism and we cosset the child. . . . Many of the child lovers are among the careless about Baptism. This is only one of several current indications how the cult of the child in the Church may destroy the worship of the Gospel; how natural religion drives out spiritual and especially evangelical. I have been at many Sunday School anniversaries and I have found the same thing shown; all the singing, even of the morning service, is on these occasions given up to childrens', not to say babies', hymns, with music to correspond, while Baptism was of little moment, or was hidden away in the home. [58]

In the above, Forsyth scathingly deplores worship which focuses upon the child rather than on what God does for the child. All of

---

[57] Karl Barth, *The Teaching of the Church Regarding Baptism,* trans. E. Payne (London: S.C.M. Press, 1945), p. 31.

[58] P. T. Forsyth, *Lectures on the Church and Sacraments* (London: Longmans, Green & Co., Ltd., 1917), pp. 171-172.

the grand arguments brought to bear for the validity of infant baptism
become ludicrous when the act is rendered inconsequential. But
Forsyth is not through; he continues, ". . . to regard Baptism as a
Sacrament, as a visible preaching of the historic word of regeneration,
as a prime part, therefore, of a Church's existence and work, and yet
to retire almost wholly when Baptism is administered . . . runs the
risk of becoming a hypocrisy." [59]

This is a welcome protest against an attitude toward baptism which
makes it separate and apart from an act of worship. It condemns
baptism that is nothing short of magic, a means of infant regeneration, in which the believing community has no stake. Dietrich Bonhoeffer indicates by implication that the problem continues for contemporary paedobaptists: "As far as infant baptism is concerned, it
must be insisted that the sacrament should be administered only
where there is a firm faith present which remembers Christ's deed
of salvation wrought for us once and for all. That can only happen
in a living Christian community. To baptize infants without a Church
is not only an abuse of the sacrament, it betokens a disgusting
frivolity in dealing with the souls of the children themselves." [60]

It is not possible to supply matching quotations arising from dis-
satisfaction on the part of churches espousing believers' baptism. In
itself, this is a telling fact. Paedobaptists, Congregationalists, or
others need not suffer from a supposed comparison with Baptists,
Disciples, and so forth. The lack of written material on the question
of baptism and worship can only mean a proportionate lack of
concern.

Here also are private baptisms. More significantly, a baptismal
service usually takes place on Sunday night if these churches meet
for worship at that time. Some churches have moved their baptistries
out of the sanctuary to more remote locations in the building. The
baptistry chapel may be so small that it accommodates only the
family and a few close friends when baptism takes place.

The decor and structure of most baptismal pools are not insig-

[59] *Ibid.*, p. 173.
[60] Dietrich Bonhoeffer, *The Cost of Discipleship* (New York: The Macmillan Co., 1961), p. 210.

nificant. Fifty years ago or more, a scene was painted on the back wall of the baptistry, depicting, more or less, the River Jordan. The fact that trees foreign to those found in the Jordan Valley frequently were shown failed to interfere with the idea that baptism should be pictured in a setting similar to environs in which Jesus was baptized. More recently, the scenic settings have often been dispensed with in favor of glass-enclosed pools. This may be due to the increasingly frequent accent on the mode of baptism rather than on its meaning. A glass front for the baptistry allows the congregation to witness that the candidate is fully immersed, because the act of immersion is in full view from start to finish. This does preclude the necessity of the practice of the Latter-day Saints, who find it necessary to have at least two elders watch the one performing the baptism, from a vantage point from which the total immersion of the candidate is made certain.

Through these windows by which one may look into the watery grave, the fact of immersion becomes so vivid that the symbol of the death and burial of the old life and resurrection to the new is not easily maintained. Similarly, baptism taking place before a backdrop on which is depicted a river connotes baptism into the same water in which Jesus was baptized, more than baptism into His death, burial, and resurrection. If, perchance, a church is lucky enough to have both a scenic mural and a transparent front, the impression of being immersed in the Jordan River is faithfully portrayed. The great theme of believers' baptism is dry-docked somewhere along the shady shore line.

Baptism has been gutted of symbolic meaning and reduced to a ceremony signifying little to anyone but the candidate. Already in competition with the powerful doctrine of personal confession and experience, baptism can do little to counterbalance the extreme individualism and subjectivism that prevail in the milieu of believers' baptism. In consequence, these churches do not thrive in the vast urban communities as they do in towns and rural areas. The heterogeneity of urbanized society defies the myriad attractions of congenial religiosity. Heterogeneous societies will continue to be indifferent to churches that either will not or cannot provide an environment conducive to the objective qualities of worship. The slow death of Baptists, Disciples, and other groups in the major cities of the Northeast is ample evidence of this fact.

7   Ecumenicity

Hopes for Christian unity are inextricably tied to the future of Christian baptism. The complicated relationship between baptism and ecumenicity, plus the baptismal problem itself, does not project an optimistic prospect. Baptism, originally an inclusive and unifying act, has become a source of exclusiveness and disunity.

The resulting anomaly should occasion little surprise. On the one hand there continues the expressed conviction that baptism holds the key to Christian unity. Other opinions are to the contrary. R. E. O. White belongs to the first persuasion: ". . . every consideration of what New Testament baptism offered to men, suggests that much of the spiritual malaise of the modern church is traceable to baptismal inadequacies. On the wider issues involved, words of J. R. C. Perkin are just: 'There can be no doubt but that sooner or later the Church will have to settle this question of baptism, which threatens to become one of the major stumbling blocks in the path of the ecumenical conversations.' " [61]

Following the pattern of American theologians' desire to undervalue the theme of baptism for the sake of ecumenicity, one may turn again—no longer with surprise—to Morrison: "By baptism is not meant immersion, nor affusion, nor any physical act whatsoever, but the moral act of uniting oneself with those who are of like mind with oneself concerning Jesus Christ. Such an act is a true moral sign of faith and repentance. Baptism, therefore, is a moral virtue. It is not a physical act; not the putting away of the filth of the flesh. It is not an outward sign." [62]

In his eagerness to promote Christian unity, Morrison resorts once more to his familiar pattern of reductionism. In making the act of

[61] R. E. O. White, *The Biblical Doctrine of Initiation* (Grand Rapids, Mich.: Wm. B. Eerdmans Publishing Co., 1960), p. 279.
[62] Charles Clayton Morrison, *The Meaning of Baptism* (Chicago: Disciples Publication Society, 1914), p. 89.

baptism irrelevant, he fails to see that an infant cannot participate in the "moral act of uniting oneself with those who are of like mind." He unwittingly obstructs his own purpose.

Nels Ferre comes closer to the present temper of tending to dismiss the question entirely from the ecumenical stage. "Jesus subordinated the Sabbath, the holy day, to man," is his enjoinder, "and then Paul made even circumcision of no effect. Paul thanked God that he did not baptize if it was to cause a division in the church. Ordinances and symbols are sacred channels when used in love by the power of the Holy Spirit. They become curses when they are made the occasion of separation or superiority. The Holy Spirit transcends all barriers to fellowship except the refusal of fellowship. That is the sin against the Holy Spirit which underlies all others. Individualism can never be forgiven; it can only be destroyed." [63]

Ferre must surely be aware that the Sabbath question, for Jesus, and the circumcision controversy, for Paul, were subordinated and made ineffectual in protest to the rigidity of Jewish legalism. It does not follow that baptism occasioned a similar protest on Paul's part. Regarding I Cor. 1:11-17, Ferre draws a similar inference to that of Brunner, but with no greater justification and with no attempt to compensate, as Brunner did (*vide* pp. 63-64). This calls for another reminder that Paul was disturbed at the factionalism evidenced in the different groups of the Corinthian Church, which had loyally clustered around their favorite ministers. Baptism had suffered a worse fate than that of theological strife and distortion. It had been made the badge of identity by which each of the schismatic groups recognized its leader. The fact that Paul did not baptize many people was possibly because local officials performed this service. The main emphasis in his reference to baptism in this instance was a feeling of relief that he had not baptized them so that they could not say they had been baptized in the name of Paul. With his profound utterances that baptism is into Christ, Paul's disparagement of baptism would be incomprehensible. Not only was he disturbed that the unity of the Church had been broken, but also that baptism had been

[63] Nels F. S. Ferre, *Pillars of Faith* (New York: Harper & Row, Publishers, 1948), p. 64.

abused in this way. He was relieved that he had not been a party to that abuse.

It is not necessary to adhere to a blind passion for ecumenicity in order to deplore the use of baptism as a distinctive element within organized Christianity. There are theological differences of weighty significance which divide us. More than a few of these differences are reflected in baptism as it is practiced by the different churches. But baptism in itself is never rightly used as a distinctive element. Its contributions are more comprehensive than those of a divisive function.

"It is highly significant both for the practical life of the Church and for the unity of the Church. In both respects the Church has suffered severely from the fact that the Christological significance of baptism has received so little attention. If all the churches were to become aware of baptism in the sense indicated above, the result would be a greater depth in the life of the Church as well as a greater manifestation of the unity of the Church." [64]

The well of baptism is deep enough for the Church to be able to afford breadth without its resulting in a drought of theological conviction and vitality. Advocates of infant baptism suffer from an improper view of the nature of the Church. Proponents of believers' baptism suffer from an improper attitude toward those who hold to the above improper view. But baptism is the practice and symbol of the Church and not of the world. Can anyone say that an infant, of believing and concerned parents, who has been baptized into a believing and concerned church, has no more in common with the Church than an infant of the unbelieving and the unconcerned? Do those who advocate believers' baptism really mean that an adult, with evident Christian convictions expressed through grand ethical ventures, has no more right to their community, because he was baptized in infancy, than the most brazen enemy of the Church? Can Christians partake of the Lord's Supper together, as is increasingly the case, and then use baptism as a means to disunity, distinctiveness, and exclusion from membership in some of the Churches? The smaller "fence" around the table cannot be removed so long as the

[64] G. H. W. Lampe and David M. Paton (eds.), *One Lord, One Baptism* (London: SCM Press, 1960), p. 71.

bigger "fence" around the churches remains. Is it not also true that paedobaptists, glorying in a cultural status consonant with the history of the established churches, refuse to accept the judgment of those whose desire to take the Church seriously brought about their social and cultural disfranchisement? Their bemused tolerance of the churches rising from the unruly but courageously sincere sectarian movements of former years is often a transparent cover for their spiritual nonchalance and careless churchmanship. Baptism, infant or believers', is our common bond. It is not the means of entering our exclusive "key clubs."

The hunger for Christian unity cannot be allayed by food only from the table of interdenominationalism. Race and class stratification produce other hungers as well. One of the patterns, which becomes clear at most ecumenical gatherings, is that the individual's vested interest in society betrays the nature and degree of his prejudices. Usually the clergy is the obstacle standing between religious pluralism and doctrinal unity that promises closer Christian ties. They recommend endless and winding theological detours. The ecumenicist is often lost or too weary to continue.

Many laymen view this spectacle with some tolerance or with mild disgust. But their placid attitude quickly changes when their own interests are involved. After all, the clergy's status cannot be separated from denominations. He may lose prestige and influence when his smaller group is absorbed by a larger one. The layman reacts with similar alacrity as an obstructionist when he is confronted by the integration of races and social classes. The Church, which he may have partially ignored, now becomes dear to him. He does not want its congeniality perturbed. The struggle for church integration in the South has revealed that Negro and white man, Christians both, fail to take the Church seriously in the conflict. The white Southerner talks of "their churches" and "our churches" and wonders audibly why "they do not stay in their churches and leave our churches alone." The Negro, for the most part, is unwilling to admit to any responsibility for this impasse. He seeks the integration of churches in the same spirit and tone that he seeks to integrate all white institutions. In claiming that the "white church" fails to be the

Church because of its segregation, he loses sight of the responsibility of the "colored churches." Thus he still speaks out of a segregated mentality, because he thinks "negatively white" and "positively colored."

Baptism offers no comprehensive answer, but does suggest possible approaches to solving the problem. The objective attitudes embraced in the churches of paedobaptism indicate movement toward integration via the route of depersonalization. The sacrament of communion, reflecting extreme objectivity, is often integrated with the assumption that one need not mix socially with his colored brother if he takes the sacrament with him. He kneels at the altar with men of every strata by forgetting that they are persons. The subjectivity of believers' baptism is more often to be found in the social room and kitchen than at the Lord's Supper. Churches of this category show less anxiety about "breaking the bread" and "drinking the cup" at the Lord's table with the dispossessed than at the prospect of eating fried chicken with them at the family-night supper. One group would "worship" with a Negro without having any fellowship with him. The other will not worship with a Negro because it is not willing to have fellowship with him.

Each group denies the baptism it professes. The rite fails to drown all the prejudices of the former man and does not connote a new person. More significant, perhaps, is the fact that baptism does not symbolize or effect the democratization of the Holy Spirit. Christians are wrong in their apparent assumption that the Spirit establishes its first beachhead on the stormy shore of our emotions. This is treacherous sand and the Spirit finds it impossible to secure a firm footing. The less conspicuous ground of the human will is the spot where the Spirit initially gains a foothold. After all, a Christian is a person whose will is not victimized by emotions but is their commander and redeemer.

Churches practicing infant baptism must sponsor all infants receiving God's prevenient grace. They cannot do this by remote control, but achieve it by means of a covenant community filled with the Spirit. Churches practicing believers' baptism ought to confront the potential believer with a strong ethical position, without which the profession and the rite mean nothing. Infant baptism serves as a symbol that there is no difference in color. Believers' baptism serves as a symbol that color makes no difference.

Chapter Five

THE RECOVERY

OF A GOOD CONSCIENCE

Not only is it easier to disagree than to agree, it is easier to identify with the diagnostician than with the therapist. Man does not really want to be God—at least not a whole God. He aspires to a halfway divinity which would authorize him to diagnose the world's wrongs and to pronounce judgment. After that he is willing to go back to being mere man, the time for answers instead of questions having arrived.

This chapter is not written with the enthusiasm of the preceding ones. I find that my plow is not so keen for the positive furrow. The reader should guard against a similar reaction, for it is necessary to make certain affirmations. The recovery of baptism's good conscience must capture our energy. Its emergence as a trustworthy clue is not a matter which can be delayed.

1   An Appeal for a Clear Conscience

"For Christ also died for our sins once and for all. He, the just, suffered for the unjust, to bring us to God."

In the body he was put to death; in the spirit he was brought to life. And in the spirit he went and made his proclamation to the imprisoned spirits. They had refused obedience long ago, while God waited patiently in the days of Noah and the building of the

160

ark, and in the ark a few persons, eight in all, were brought to safety through the water. This water prefigured the water of baptism through which you are now brought to safety. Baptism is not the washing away of bodily pollution, but the appeal made to God by a *good conscience;* and it brings salvation through the resurrection of Jesus Christ, who entered heaven after receiving the submission of angelic authorities and powers, and is now at the right hand of God.[1]

Both *The Interpreter's Bible* and *The Interpreter's Dictionary of the Bible* prefer the translation, "the appeal made to God by a good conscience" to that of the Revised Standard Version, "an appeal to God for a clear conscience." In the latter version, baptism would mean an appeal to God by baptism resulting in His gift of a good conscience to us. The former rendering would mean that baptism is itself the act of a good conscience.

"No certainty is possible,"

. . . but the choice seems to lie between (a) a prayer to God for a good conscience; and (b) a pledge to God proceeding from a clear conscience. The first *a* may be interpreted to mean the prayer, appeal, or request which the baptized person makes to God for a good conscience. But *b* is to be preferred, and the explanation is to be found in the practice of the baptismal vows. . . . It could thus apply to the Christian's formal "confession" of his faith. We have to think of some solemn interrogatory before baptism, "Do you believe . . . and will you promise to renounce . . . ?" The whole proceeding of question and answer could thus be summarily called "a pledge to God proceeding from a clear conscience." [2]

Simon Peter, the author of this scripture, is hardly the last word on baptism among New Testament writers. There are those, in fact,

---

[1] I Pet. 3:18-22 (The New English Bible New Testament).
[2] *The Interpreter's Bible* (Nashville, Tenn.: Abingdon Press, 1957), XII, 134.

who suggest that Simon Peter did not actually baptize Cornelius, the Gentile, nor even have an associate perform the rite. This interpretation is based on the conference in which Simon Peter, defending his action to the circumcision party, does not specifically say that he baptized the centurion: "And I remembered the word of the Lord, how he said, 'John baptized with water, but you shall be baptized with the Holy Spirit.' If then God gave the same gift to them as he gave to us when we believed in the Lord Jesus Christ, who was I that I could withstand God?" [3]

These words entail something more than an exegetical gem for cutting and polishing. The possibility that Peter easily dispensed with the act of baptism with respect to Cornelius has its bearing upon the significance of the act as integral to conversion itself. Fortunately, we are able to offer a logical explanation for Peter's failure, not only at this meeting but later at the Jerusalem conference, to mention the baptism of Cornelius. The apostolic church was confronted by two problems with respect to the Gentiles. One was admission of Gentiles into the Church. The other was that of social intercourse, involving ceremonial regulations, such as the eating of certain foods. The second matter was the main ground of contention between the circumcision party and the Apostle. "Why did you go to uncircumcised men and eat with them?" was its direct inquiry. Since baptism was not being discussed, there was no reason for Peter to defend this action at this time.

Finally, Simon Peter's baptismal definition in his first letter is not out of line with his admonition at Pentecost that the new converts should "repent, and be baptized every one of you in the name of Jesus Christ for the forgiveness of your sins; and you shall receive the gift of the Holy Spirit." [4] Care is called for in the apparent association of baptism and the forgiveness of sins. The association between repentance and forgiveness is as clearly attested to, perhaps more so. Nevertheless, Peter's call for baptism for everyone must stand.

[3] Acts 11:16-17.
[4] Acts 2:38.

With these explanations at hand, we may proceed with a clear conscience to speak of baptism as the "appeal of a good conscience to God." The definitions of baptism are not hereby exhausted. However, in this wise, baptism connotes man's open, honest, and communal response to God's salvation. He has done what he ought to have done. His confession is neither in the secret recesses of his own being nor among the nameless benefits of ethical conduct. Between these poles, he has taken upon himself a name. That name is "Christian." As one joins with the community of the Lord, the fruits of the Spirit, ethically expressed, are borne in the name of Christ. J. B. Denny's dictum is apt: "Baptism and faith are but the outside and the inside of the same thing." [5] Faith is baptism's reason for being. Baptism is faith's expression.

The recovery of a good conscience, in respect to baptism, calls for a confession by the churches of their frivolous and careless use of the rite. Coupled with confession must be a sober and earnest attempt to find and employ an authentic Christian baptism from a blend of the New Testament witness and its subsequent theology; the latter must provide answers to questions which are neither asked nor answered in the New Testament. With this end in view,

> We are faced then with a form of baptism in the modern church very unlike that of the New Testament in form, content, and theological significance, yet enshrining certain values and insights which in any final appraisal of the rite (or rapprochement among the churches) must be preserved and prized. If infant baptism witnesses to them in a confused and ambiguous way, believers' baptism also may sometimes obscure them altogether. If it be asked, why, then, both forms of baptism may not exist side by side in the modern church, the answer must be, first, that all our study has shown that New Testament Baptism possessed a richness of meaning which neither current practice commonly possesses—and to

_____

[5] I cannot locate the primary source. The secondary source is *The Interpreter's Dictionary of the Bible* (Nashville, Tenn.: Abingdon Press, 1962), I, 351.

maintain two impaired baptisms does nothing toward recovering biblical initiation.[6]

White makes a sound and sensible plea. He does not insist that the New Testament is the sole guide to the meaning of baptism. Although baptism in the modern church is unlike New Testament baptism, it does have some values which ought to be preserved. These qualities are supplementary to those which are both explicit and implicit within New Testament scripture. They are supplementary because they deal with post-New Testament conditions and situations. Some values of modern baptism do not appear in the New Testament because there was no place for them at the time. The changing Church in a changing culture is the basis for their appearance and a testimony to their importance. At the same time, there is much in contemporary baptism that does not supplement the New Testament view but which defies and controverts it. "Peaceful coexistence" of the two main forms, which some wish for and promote, is not advisable. This is not because the wish is impossible, but because of the need for continuing judgment upon the doctrine and practice of each.

The means of arriving at a definition and description of Christian baptism must therefore be faithful to the New Testament. Scripture can neither be ignored nor contradicted in this regard. Whatever theology for baptism arises without benefits of the New Testament witness must be true to its general principles, although it may not be directly indebted to any particular word of the text. Present theology ought to be closely examined so as to divide the chaff from the wheat, as far as baptism is concerned. A definition of Christian baptism does not demand new content so much as a vigorous and courageous re-examination of the content which already exists.

2   Christian Baptism as Christian Initiation

Baptism is Christian initiation. One grants that this is not too well attested by the New Testament. One grants that the New Testament

[6] R. E. O. White, *The Biblical Doctrine of Initiation* (Grand Rapids, Mich.: Wm. B. Eerdmans Publishing Co., 1960), pp. 295-296.

speaks of baptism into Christ, into the Trinity, into His body, and into His Spirit, but not into the Church. One grants also that the Church today is at many points sub-Christian, unlike the New Testament in numerous ways—an institution with every sin besides, in comparison with the loosely knit but dynamic and faithful fellowship of the New Testament.

This is the only Church there is, and baptism is its means of enrollment. Otherwise, membership is dependent upon the edict of a special priesthood, graduation from a catechismal school, or the majority vote of the people. None of these is reflective of Christian theology to an appreciable degree. Baptism, however, spells out personal faith and confession; the work of God in the giving of the Spirit and salvation; the glorifying of God in the atoning death and triumphant resurrection of Christ the Lord; death to sin and the newness of life to come; cleansing for ethical and moral life; identification with the death, burial, and resurrection of Christ; and a community of faith as the arena of the Spirit's visitation upon the one whose faith has brought him to the water.

We may wish to support Denny's view that "the earliest creed, if one may call it so, was involved in the baptismal formula: the name of the Father, the Son, and the Holy Spirit, comprehends all that is distinctive in Christianity. But in a philosophising environment, where persons and facts became ideas, and ideas abstractions, this was not enough; and the baptismal confession was expanded into a rule of faith, for which apostolic authority was claimed." [7]

Denny's concern is justified. The symbolic formula by which one was baptized into Father, Son, and Holy Spirit became a thing in itself. Initiation was not into Jesus Christ, Son of God, by His Spirit. It became initiation into a doctrine or an idea. Baptism was robbed of personality and spirit in the interval. This is not pure baptism. It is a perversion of the act in both faith and practice. The answer is not, however—and Denny does not so imply—to establish a substitute for baptism, but to correct the distortion so that baptism may be true to its own nature. Nor does the probable fact that distortion

[7] James Denny, *Studies in Theology* (London: Hodder and Stoughton, 1906), p. 193.

will never be completely eliminated indicate that baptism should be disparaged and cast aside as meaningless. The only course open is the practice of baptism with the knowledge that man distorts all things and must move on with the "courage of imperfection," accepting as one the judgment and redemptive love of God.

Others who rule out baptism as Christian initiation, not on the basis of the rite but because of the body into which one is baptized, may also turn to Denny. Speaking of the Church, he says:

> It is no longer the fellowship of the saints, the community of those who possess salvation in Jesus Christ; it is the community which confesses certain historical facts, and recognizes certain interpretations of them, and a certain collection of writings, not perfectly definite indeed, as religiously authoritative. The spiritual character of the Church has retired, and it has assumed an intellectual aspect. I do not mean that the Christianity of it has been lost; nay, it was an active effort of the Christianity within the Church which set up the rule of faith and the canon of the New Testament in self-defence. It was well meant, and it was well done, but it shifted the emphasis in the conception of the Church, and we have had to pay for that ever since.[8]

This sounds like much of the criticism now leveled at the Church. If so, Denny is in accord with those who would do away with the Church entirely or those who wish to go back to cells of Christianity. This is because they gather those of like mind to whom mutual fellowship is easy but fellowship with the world impossibly difficult.

Emil Brunner, it appears, would not disagree with Denny's version of the shifted emphasis regarding the conception of the Church. At the same time, he takes care to make sure that the "Body of Christ," which is called the "Ecclesia," is not understood as something apart and different, in any unequivocal sense, from what we commonly call the Church. The price we pay, to paraphrase Denny's lament, is the price of knowing the connection between the Church and the "Body of Christ," as well as the difference.

[8] *Ibid.*, pp. 194-195.

Although every Church must realize that it serves to build up the "Body of Christ" instead of being the "Body," Brunner favors baptism as the means for incorporation and enrollment into the Church. Conversion is both the disintegration of the old man and the integration of the new. This is not merely integration of the new person, however, but also "integration into the fellowship, or the integration of fellowship." Brunner goes on to say that "the solitary man, who is most profoundly isolated by sin from his fellow man, is incorporated into the fellowship of faith of the Ecclesia and thus becomes a member of the new humanity. This also happens in a corresponding personal event, in a two-sided act. In the New Testament this act is Baptism, and just for this reason it is so intimately bound up in the New Testament witness with rebirth. . . . Through Baptism the spiritual and personal event becomes at the same time a spiritual and social event.[9]

A supporting word for his final sentence above is offered in the comment "that in the nature of things the Ecclesia is both an invisible spiritual reality and a visible social reality. The Body of Christ is at once something which can be apprehended only by faith and something which is visible even to the unbeliever as a social fact." [10]

Before we pick out our religious "ingroup," let us at least remember that any historical and theological connection between the Church now and the Church of the New Testament authenticates, to the degree there is a connection, the contemporary institution. Baptism counters many of our choice invectives against the institutional Church. No one can be baptized into the "pure Church" unless he is baptized into the Church as it now stands.

It is true that the Church has "paid the price," because it tried to be the Church by adopting a rule of faith and canonizing the Gospel. Every Christian movement in history has demonstrated the same pattern. Each discipleship knew what it was trying to be and why. The apostolic Church enjoyed this awareness. But when it—and all

---

[9] Emil Brunner, *The Christian Doctrine of the Church, Faith and the Consummation,* trans. David Cairns in collaboration with T. H. L. Parker (Philadelphia: The Westminster Press, 1962), III, "Dogmatics," 274.

[10] *Ibid.,* p. 43.

subsequent movements—tried to explain itself to the world, it became encumbered with institutionalized practices.

The institutional Church is not the body of Christ. But it serves
to build up the "body." We cannot deny that we torture the body
in the process and cause it undue pain. By our own doing, there is
no perfect Church. We continue to skeptically finger and pick at the
scars of the crucified body, trying to prove the reality of the cross.
But they are scars—wounds healed over! The crucifixion of Christ
is a finished work. Our probing fingers are unclean, but they cannot
infect. Where do these criticisms of the Church come from?
Largely, they come from the Church itself. Seldom—if at all—has
the world leveled an accusation at the Church that has not already
been painfully discussed in many groups within the Church.

The remedy does not lie with tabulating assets and liabilities. To
talk about "what's right with the Church" as a counterbalance to
"what's wrong with the Church" would be a futile gallimaufry. The
Church's witness to the world, without and within, will make far
greater impact when it acts on the forgiveness it has received instead
of working for forgiveness by incessantly confessing its sins.

Baptism may be defective as its means of incorporation, and may
carry over defection into the membership. Nevertheless, any form
of baptism, however improper, is Christian initiation. This conviction
is supplementary to the New Testament evidence. It could be no
other way. The New Testament did not envision baptism as enrollment into an institution because it did not foresee the Church in
institutional terms. Baptism into the name of Christ antedated baptism into His body, which the Church supports. It is the present responsibility of all Christian churches to settle this primary question.
To whatever extent a church is of the Church, its members should
have been received by the act of baptism. This must be asserted no
matter what one church may think of the baptism of another. Here
is common ground on which the Church may stand as that company
which is not of the world although it is in the world. For the purpose
of this point at least, it is irrelevant to discuss how much difference,
how much impact, baptism makes as far as the individual is con-

cerned. We may be sure of this: baptism can make little difference to the person if it makes little difference to the Church. It is first the responsibility of the Church to be serious about the act by which it incorporates its members. Let other responsibilities be confronted as they arise consequent to resolution of the primary consideration.

3 Baptism as a Symbol

James Cleland, preacher to Duke University and Dean of the Chapel, has often wished for a third word between ordinance and sacrament in the vocabulary of the Reformed tradition. As for the dictionary's meaning of the terms, he feels that each says something important while leaving much unsaid which ought to be said. This is a legitimate wish and makes sense if one is forced to choose between the two. The word "sacrament," popularly defined, harbors a magic which cannot be drowned or made obsolete, no matter what the protestations are to the contrary. The word "ordinance" is bereft of mystery. It has no place for God or his work. It is man's obedience to Christ's memorandum, which He left behind, tacked on the bulletin board of scripture.

It is appropriate that baptism renders both words unsatisfactory. It is not an ordinance, a sign, that man is mimicking Jesus or doing what God commanded. There is no sign by which man may signify his obedience to God. Every command of God, whether it be the Decalogue or the positive orders of the New Testament, involves man in ethical action that is continuous rather than a finished, final act. Man is not able to stand away from his obedience and point to it with a sign. He cannot objectify his love by signifying it as a thing apart. Ordinances are necessary for the purposes of a structured society. They have a valid place in any community. They are not relevant to the dynamic and personal relationship, however, between God and persons in or out of the community.

Baptism is not a sacrament, because it does not work independently of conscious persons. It does not possess within itself, apart from believing individuals, any degree of power. Power resides neither in the water nor the act. Neither does the rite provide a visible setting in which God offers invisible grace. This would suggest opening the curtain on a visible stage while the audience deludes itself that something real is happening which cannot be seen.

A choice between the two concepts is neither inevitable nor necessary. There is a word for baptism which is obvious and time-honored rather than being unique and novel. Symbol is the word. Symbolically, it holds all the mystery innately belonging to the rite. By "mystery," we do not mean a plot to unravel, a secret to disclose, or a riddle to solve. The mystery of God is a part of His revelation. When it is revealed, it does not cease to be mystery. It is an "open secret." Mystery and revelation are intertwined. For there are those who "seeing do not see" and who "hearing do not hear." The concept of the "spiritual" has suffered the misfortune of acquiring pietistic and sanctimonious connotations. The resulting substitution of spatial and sensory terms as definitive is misleading and harmful. Inevitably, we are conditioned to use such words as "inner" and "outer" or "invisible" and "visible" in dealing with the work and community of the Spirit. Confusion occurs when the spiritual work and community is confined to that which is inner and invisible. The Holy Spirit should not be relegated to a dimension which is always interior and invisible. What is seen is then automatically interpreted as a sign that points to the interior and invisible Spirit. The Spirit, in this sense, has no part in the sign or act which it creates. Baptism, as a symbol of the revealed mystery, does not imply that it has an inner and invisible meaning which is not present in the outer and visible act.

Brunner believes that baptism, for Paul, was the visible happening of what had already happened invisibly "through the Word and faith." It was not a significant factor in man's salvation in any other sense than bringing to sight what was unseen.[11] He takes the trouble, however, to elaborate on the doctrine of baptism from Paul's comprehensive view of faith. In doing so, the concept of "mystery" is used to telling advantage. After declaring that baptism is indigenous

---

[11] Emil Brunner, *The Christian Doctrine of the Church, Faith, and the Consummation,* trans. David Cairns in collaboration with T. H. L. Parker (Philadelphia: The Westminster Press, 1962), III, "Dogmatics," 42.

to "saving history," Brunner observes that baptism belongs to an Ecclesia which is both aware of the redemption that happened in Jesus and of its own upbuilding by the Spirit of God in the community of faith. The failure of the Church to evidence this in faith and practice corresponds to the failure of the Church to be the Ecclesia instead of being wholly institutional in form and mentality. Baptismal doctrines have consequently been, "in one way or another, unsatisfying, unconvincing and contradictory." [12]

It may safely be assumed that so long as the institutional Church insists upon spelling out the rite of baptism in terms of dogma, practice, and form, these undesirable conditions will continue. Baptism is a "revealed mystery" and the more it is known the greater its mystery.

Turning again to Brunner: "In this oldest primitive Christian rite, taken already for granted in the Ecclesia and by it traced back to the command of Jesus to baptize, the feeling is concealed that in all the working of the Holy Spirit through the divine Word a mystery is to be guarded that cannot be expressed in any doctrine, the secret working of the Holy Spirit, which as such transcends all theological understanding and must be 'left in situ' by us simply as a mystery." [13]

Granting the necessary use of spatial and sensory words, baptism's mystery is not eliminated by its becoming outer and visible. Discernment is spiritually determined. Whatever happens in baptism does not only happen apart from or behind the act: it also happens in the act. Nor is the meaning of the act hidden like a label on the inner lining of a coat. Baptism need not be turned inside out as a means to its understanding.

The teaching Spirit does not make the invisible visible, but reveals the mystery. The means of this revealing is symbolization. In Christian experience the symbol is an encounter between teaching Spirit and believing man, between coming Spirit and responding man. When one is baptized, he, the baptizer, and the believing congregation both behold and participate in a mystery. Baptism into God—Father, Son, and Spirit—into the death, burial, and resurrection of

---

[12] *Ibid.*, pp. 56-57.
[13] *Ibid.*, p. 57.

our Lord, into the believing community, can never actually achieve visibility in the strictest sense of the word. It is spiritually discerned because it is Spirit-given.

Paul Tillich's rich definition of the nature of the symbol undergirds the connection between it and mystery. Concerning our aversion to the use of sensory and spatial concepts for divine mystery, it is helpful to read Tillich's distinction between general and religious symbolism. After asserting that religious symbolism combines all that is characteristic of the symbol in general, he understands a religious symbol to represent a reality which can never be completely known. "Religious symbols," he says, "represent the transcendent but do not make the transcendent immanent. They do not make God a part of the empirical world." [14]

Those characteristics belonging both to general and religious symbols are illuminating for the purpose at hand. The first two mentioned by Tillich are self-explanatory.

The first and basic characteristic of a symbol is its figurative quality. . . . The second characteristic of the symbol is its perceptibility. . . . The third characteristic of the symbol is its innate power. This implies that the symbol has a power inherent within it that distinguishes it from the mere sign which is impotent in itself. This characteristic is the most important one. It gives to the symbol the reality which it has lost in ordinary usage, as the phrase "only a symbol" shows. This characteristic is decisive for the distinction between a sign and symbol. The sign is interchangeable at will. It does not arise from necessity, for it has no inner power. The symbol, however, does possess a necessary character. It cannot be exchanged. It can only disappear, when, through dissolution, it loses its inner power. Nor can it be merely construed, it can only be created. . . . The fourth characteristic of the symbol is its acceptability as such. This implies that the symbol is socially rooted and socially supported. . . . The act by

[14] Rollo May (ed.), *Symbolism in Religion and Literature* (New York: George Braziller, Inc., 1960), chap. 2, "The Religious Symbol," by Paul Tillich, p. 77.

which a symbol is created is a social act, even though it first springs forth in an individual. The individual can devise signs for his own private needs; he cannot make symbols.[15]

The third and most important characteristic mentioned by Tillich undergirds the argument of this book. A symbol is not exchangeable. It possesses a necessary character in relation to the reality it represents. Neither the symbol nor the reality it conveys can be tampered with without damaging one or the other. The Church for generations has not been mindful of this fact. It has assumed that it could change one without affecting the other. The resulting confusion and chaos is sufficient evidence of its grievous error. Loss of power accurately describes the plight of baptism's symbol in our time.

Tillich's fourth point is also decisive. The social acceptability of a symbol is necessary to its place and function in religious life. Neither an individual nor an institution may arbitrarily decide that a symbol conveying one truth to society in general may mean something else in personal or private terms. That would destroy the communicative role of the symbol. For example, baptism in history has stood for Christian initiation, not only to those in the Church but to those in the world. Endeavors to make it mean something else, for personal and expedient reasons, threaten its symbolic power altogether.

The function of the symbol of baptism is not unlimited in scope. Three statements serve to clarify its limits: (a) The act of baptism symbolizes baptism into Christ and His body which the Church serves. It is identification with Christ and the community of His Spirit. (b) One may identify with Christ without baptism. Hence it is not a sacrament. (c) However, a person can hardly identify with the Church or symbolize that identification in the world without baptism. Baptism is the only symbol at hand. It is the given symbol by which the Spirit interprets the mystery to the spiritually discerning. Furthermore, it speaks its message to the world in the only language that the world can understand.

There is danger in the desire for a more explicit description of the symbol of baptism than has been given here. This desire appears

[15] *Ibid.*, pp. 75-76.

more often among those who deplore sacramentalism than among those who are openly sacramental in their views. The term "prophetic symbolism" is used by theologians wishing to avoid the pitfalls of sacramentalism while they give the baptismal symbol more status. A New Testament scholar puts it in this way: "There was nothing magical in the community's practice of baptism: it did not effect a moral change in the person baptized. It was a symbolic act, like those performed by the Old Testament prophets and men of God. Such acts not only symbolized what prophets declared would come to pass, but were believed to help bring about what was prophesied. For example, Moses raised his hand over warring Israel not merely as a sign that the nation would triumph, but as a human channel through which God could work to give Israel the victory." [16]

Rejecting prophetic symbolism does not mean a simultaneous rejection of God's using human instruments for His purpose. However, the doctrine comes close to the sacramentalism for which it proposes a substitute. The idea that the prophetic symbol helps to bring about the purpose of God will inevitably degenerate into the assumption that it helps God where He needs help. Finally, it imprisons God. It is the way of Elijah who poured water on the altar wood, in contrast to the dry timber of the prophets of Baal, and put God in a strait where He had no choice but to burn the wood. That He did not burn Elijah at the same time is testimony to His grace. There is too little difference between prophetic symbolism and sacramentalism to justify the use of separate terms.

"The act of baptism," it is far better said,

proves to be the meeting place of divine and human activity; it becomes the objective vehicle alike of the convert's penitent resolve and of the divine remission and acceptance. But this is a mode of divine-human relationship which needs neither prophetic symbolism, supernaturalism nor sacramentalism to explain it: essentially, it is the simple evangelical truth of divine accessibility to every trembling approach of man, the certainty that he who asks

[16] Howard Kee and Franklin Young, *Understanding the New Testament* (Englewood Cliffs, N.J.: Prentice-Hall, Inc., 1957), p. 187.

does receive, that they that seek invariably find, and that there is
joy in heaven over one sinner that repenteth.[17]

4   The Proper Subjects for Baptism

The assertion that baptism is the symbol of Christian initiation
leads to a difficult but inevitable question: Who are the proper subjects for baptism? The nature of the Church, God's active grace, and
man's responsibility are immediately involved.

Concerning the first point, the use of the word Ecclesia is not
in itself any guarantee of a fundamental quality of the Church.

"Ecclesia was used primarily to designate a particular communal
reality, not to describe its qualitative aspects. Where the distinctive
qualities and dimensions of community life were intended, other
terms proved more flexible and evocative. In comparison with these
other terms, ecclesia was relatively neutral and colorless, conveying
by itself little theological meaning. It was open to use, without basic
shift in meaning, by unbelievers as well as by believers." [18]

The basic meaning of the word in the Old Testament is a meeting
or a gathering. In the New Testament it could mean a gathering for
a particular purpose, a community of believers within a given area,
a community called out by God through Christ, or the eschatological
people of God.[19] The determinant for the nature of the Church,
therefore, is the Risen Lord and the responding community. The
Church takes none of its primary characteristics from the initiative
of man. Whatever human characteristics are found in the Church
are necessarily responses to the Spirit of the Risen Lord. Christ is
the foundation of the Church. The Church builds His body. He is
head of the body. While responding persons are not primary in the
Church, they are nonetheless necessary. There is no proper Church
without a surrendered people who have been called to commitment
through Christ.

[17] R. E. O. White, *The Biblical Doctrine of Initiation* (Grand Rapids, Mich.:
Wm. B. Eerdmans Publishing Co., 1960), p. 87.

[18] *The Interpreter's Dictionary of the Bible* (Nashville, Tenn.: Abingdon
Press, 1962), I, 607.

[19] *Ibid.*, p. 608.

God's grace and man's personal response are the two fundamental acts necessary to the Church. Infant baptism excludes the second factor. Believers' baptism does not exclude God's grace but tends to obscure it by an inordinate accent upon man's act of faith. It is fair to say that believers' baptism is indigenous to the time and place of the Reformation rather than being a distinctive New Testament characteristic. The practice arose as a necessary corrective to the Roman Catholic doctrine of baptism coupled with the failure of the Reformation principals to seek a definitive doctrine and practice of baptism commensurate with the Reformation principle.

This implies difficulty in determining the proper subjects for baptism because the relationship of faith and grace has already been subjected to a varied plethora of pressures. Direct appeal to the New Testament does not promise an early end to the reigning uncertainty. It is conclusive that the theology of the New Testament disfavors infant baptism with considerable inflexibility. On the other hand, the New Testament evidence for the practice of infant baptism cannot be summarily dismissed as an "argument from silence." The assumption that persons born of Christian parents were not baptized until they had reached the age of discretion or accountability must also be argued from silence. A second complication is the assured impossibility of recapturing the New Testament Church without abolishing the form and institution of the Church as it now is. The only workable option is to find the proper subjects of baptism for the contemporary Church within a grace-faith context while looking to the New Testament as the most resourceful guide.

In this perspective, notwithstanding his avowed suspicion of infant baptism, Brunner freely contends that "baptism in particular is the event which points to the grace and the prevenience of Him Who is the foundation of the Church. In this sense even Infant Baptism could be acknowledged and rightly administered, as the sign that points to Him, His grace which precedes all preaching and all faith." [20]

---

[20] Emil Brunner, *The Christian Doctrine of the Church, Faith, and the Consummation,* trans. David Cairns in collaboration with T. H. L. Parker (Philadelphia: The Westminster Press, 1962), III, 57.

(Baptism before faith is not in correspondence with the grace-faith formula necessary to the Church and to its means of initiation and incorporation. This concept is contradictory to the New Testament theology which Brunner relies upon. He is much closer to reality when he explicates the practice of the New Testament church. He avers: "Especially in the true Ekklesia, parents who believed in Christ must have placed their children who as yet did not understand a single word under the hand of blessing of Him who is 'the Father of every family in heaven and on earth' (Eph. 3:15) in the certainty that as to believers, so also to their children, His grace and His loving Fatherhood is assured in Jesus Christ, with the prayer to fulfil this promise. They also wished that His name should be joined with the name of this child of theirs and that it should thereby be placed under His power and His protection." [21]

The claim that this is closer to reality does not necessarily sanction it as recommended practice for baptism.

It does suggest that parental concern and brooding faith of this nature are at once understandable and informative. Whatever it may lack in terms of personal responsibility is balanced by a theological understanding of the nature of God, given expression in Jesus Christ. It serves to bring into full view the faith-work formula, the harsh legalism of which is often so intrinsic an element in believers' baptism as to be hidden from casual eyes. The practice of infant baptism would alter the principal motif of the Church from the direction of the certainty of sin toward that of mercy and loving kindness. Then it may quit its busy testing and measuring in order to prove itself and practice the proof of a loving God.

This is as far as we can take the matter.(A personal God moves toward relationship with persons) His grace does not sit imprisoned in the cubicle of an automat, its locked doors waiting to be sprung by feeding the sacramental slot while He remains anonymous behind the façade. The faith-response of man is what God intends. Faith, it should be said, unlocks no more doors than sacrament; it is not a key to anything. It is neither knowledge nor wisdom. It is not a leap into the abyss, presupposing an unseen net below. It is not

[21] *Ibid.,* p. 57.

betting one's life that there is a God. It is not a whistling walk
through darkness nor the lighting of a candle. There is already a
light which the darkness has not and cannot overcome. Faith is the
affirmation of that light. Faith is not an embrace of dogma nor a
stubborn conviction about things unproved. Faith is response, in
surrender and gratitude, to God's loving. It is not predicated upon
what is to be but what already is. Faith is the act of a trusting person.

"Truly, I say to you, whoever does not receive the kingdom of
God like a child shall not enter it." [22] Significantly enough, the
staunchest paedobaptist scholars give little attention to this verse
nestled in the Scriptures from which they infer support for infant
baptism. This is the better part of wisdom. The verse indicates the
manner of receiving the kingdom of God rather than the manner in
which Christ and His Church receive infants. The fact that Luke's
account substitutes infants for children is not sufficient evidence to
counteract the implication that the children of the narrative were
old enough to make some response to Jesus Christ. *The Interpreter's
Bible* is convinced that the "relevance of vs. 15 in the present context
is indubitable. Much of Jesus' ministry was concerned with awakening men to responsiveness; much of the opposition to him came from
those who lacked imagination, receptivity, and the childlike capacity
to act at once upon what they understood—held fast as they were
in their adult skepticisms and misgivings." [23]

So long as the manner of receiving Christ and His kingdom is a
legitimate element in the Marcan passage, its use in support of the
doctrine of infant baptism is problematical. Many advocating believers' baptism reject the faintest suggestion that the passage has
any reference, directly or indirectly, to baptism of any kind. They
prefer to interpret it with Matthew 18:2-4 and Mark 9:36. In each
of these instances, the emphasis is upon humility. In the first instance,
the spirit in which we enter the kingdom of heaven is underscored.
In the second, humility as the ground of true greatness is proclaimed.
These emphases do not coincide with the childlikeness that is focal

[22] Mark 10:15.
[23] *The Iinterpreter's Bible* (Nashville, Tenn.: Abingdon Press, 1957), VII,
800.

in Mark 10:13-16. Here the qualities of dependence, spontaneity, and receptivity are central.[24]

The passage, as it stands, deals a crippling blow to paedobaptism. Infants are not proper subjects for baptism since they are incapable of response and reception where both are necessary. At the same time, the passage causes grave difficulty for those who are the sternest proponents of believers' baptism. The doctrine of the latter casts suspicion upon the baptism of a child. It fails to acknowledge that if one must be like a child in receiving and entering the kingdom, then a child can, in his own right, receive and enter the kingdom. If the choice between infants and believers is forced, then believers must be given precedence as the subjects of baptism. However, when faith accents man's believing in a sense that seems indigenous to believers' baptism, it comes perilously close to being a "work." Faith is no longer faith, but becomes a new kind of legalism and "work." Humility about a "faith-work" may be a gratifying goal for those who sponsor the cause of believers' baptism. But this is not sufficient to prevent faith from becoming a "work" where faith is unduly exaggerated. Dependence, receptivity, and spontaneous trust are the elements of faith which keep it pure. The flaw in the doctrine and practice of believers' baptism from the Reformation until now is that the kind of faith it deems absolutely necessary to baptism hinders, if not prevents, the believer from achieving the pure faith he is supposed to have. It must follow, therefore that a person fully indoctrinated by the concept of believers' baptism is less prepared for baptism than a child.

The Revised Standard Version's choice of the word "hinder" instead of "forbid" is a happy one. The original allows either. Believers' baptism, faithfully exercised, is a hindrance to the baptism of children. It has been previously noted that the most popular way of dealing with this obstacle to the baptism of children is by denying the importance of baptism. Many churches try to convince themselves that children are believers by subjecting them to a question-and-answer examination; this also is a ludicrous practice: God is understood in juvenile terms and this limitation is never overcome. The spectacle of intelli-

[24] *Ibid.*

gent men no longer concerned with the Church, denying the God of their childish mentality, is a comic tragedy. This frequently happens when churches have caricatured Him by their manipulation of a child into a "believer." The child's response to the Spirit of the Risen One must not be hindered by a forced insistence that he know intellectually "what he is doing." The important element for the child and the true Church is that the response he makes is his personal response. That response belongs to the act of baptism rather than to a subsequent rite, for example, confirmation. Dix's observation that the Church can afford infant baptism as an abnormality if it will employ the corrective of confirmation does not merit a carte blanche agreement. If faith-response is necessary to baptism, it ought to occur in the act itself.

The removal of suspicion from the baptism of a child will never be complete until the question of necessity for a conscious and deliberate confession of sin is resolved. The insistence that a child know himself as a willful sinner warrants more attention than can be given it within the limited scope of this book, but nevertheless it will be possible to illuminate the subject to some extent. There is a clue in the history of the Judaeo-Christian tradition; it rests in the fact that the Gospel is first to the Jew. John's call to repentance at the Jordan enraged the Jew, who by virtue of knowing the law, believed that only the Gentile stood in need of repentance. Jesus' encounter with the Canaanite or Syrophoenician woman is admittedly hard to understand or interpret. But we cannot evade the attestation of both Matthew (15:21-28) and Mark (7:24-30) that he was "sent only to the lost sheep of the house of Israel" and that "the children [must] first be fed." Paul, whose mission was to the Gentiles, made no effort to change the direction or priority of the gospel. "For I am not ashamed of the gospel:" he wrote in Romans, "it is the power of God for salvation to every one who has faith, to the Jew first and also to the Greek." [25]

A child of Christian parents, or one who has grown up under the ministering hand of the Church, is in an analogous position to a child of ancient Israel. This is so because he is in the tradition of

[25] Rom. 1:16.

the New Israel, i.e., the Church. As one already identified with the community of the redeemed and with the instrument of redemption, he should not be identified with the present world any more than a first-century New Israelite could be identified with the world of the Gentile. His baptism represents his conversion from the self-righteousness of a "life under law," just as the baptism of the Jew represented a similar conversion.

What God denied in Eden seems to have been supplied on Mt. Sinai. Thereupon, man learned the distinction between good and evil and presumed that he had become able to live accordingly. This presumption, while possibly delivering the Jew from unrighteousness, made him vulnerable to self-righteousness. His conversion within this state of affairs was actually salvation from legalism. The same is true for the child who is born into the tradition of the New Israel. To know himself as a conscious and deliberate sinner is an impossibility. He has been taught the love of God and the necessity of his own good as gratitude from the time that he was teachable. His conversion, therefore, is from the legalism which is necessarily implicit and explicit in all Christian education for children. It is wrong to suppose that this legalism is altogether bad. "This does not mean that the law is contrary to God's purpose. On the contrary, by the law God purposes to block up every other way except the way of grace and faith; to drive us to Christ." [26]

The incompatibility between believers' baptism and Christian education for prebaptized children has been underscored. The abolishment of Christian education is not even an option. This the Church will not and should not do. There is a connection between the selection of the child as the proper subject for Christian baptism and the prospect for the continuing predominance of Christian education within the Church ministry. Christian education cannot be separated from Judaism and its legalistic effects. The end result of Christian education, without the interruption of conversion, is the formulation of an intellectually achieved and legalistically applied ethic.

Postponement of baptism, until adolescence or later maturity, for

[26] Lesslie Newbigin, *The Household of God* (New York: Friendship Press, 1954), p. 38.

those who have been influenced by the dominant motif of Christian education is unwise. The individual under these conditions will probably be religiously structured so that he will be sinfully proud of his "theological faith" and his "legalistic goodness." This structure can become so rigid as to desensitize him to a gospel of grace. The evangelist knows that the brazen sinner of the world is often more susceptible to the "good news" than is the "good" adult who has been in Church since his infancy. If and when baptism and church membership are offered him, the latter may counter with the well-worn rejoinder: "I am as good, if not better, that most of the members of the church. Why should I be baptized and join with them?"

The baptism of the child who is old enough to be capable of personal response is the best guarantee for avoiding the profound and unyielding rigidity of legalism. This approach is not influenced by an accent on grace in contrast to the helplessness of an infant. Helplessness has nothing to do with age in terms of salvation. Helplessness is a result of sin; the older a person grows, the more helpless he may be. This concept is sure to draw an accusation that the conversion of children is one of the main causes of the nominal Christianity characterizing church members in our time. Such criticism depends upon an oversimplified analysis of the many causes for nominal Christianity. A child's baptism ought not mark the final event in his Christian education. Instead, it should be an interruption of the Christian education so that the child may respond, personally and accountably, to God's grace which has been presupposed throughout the process. This interruption has to be consciously perceived. Grace, already given in the death, burial, and resurrection of Christ, needs to be symbolized in an event that may be continuously remembered by the child. Baptism is the event and Christian education provides the memory and recall that is necessary. Nominal Christianity is more likely the result, under these circumstances, of the failure to extend the process of Christian education than of the baptism of children. The finality of Christ's saving act in history should not be construed as certainty of a corresponding finality in man's salvation.

W. D. Davies, interpreting Paul's doctrine and use of baptism, illustrates what may be used in analogy to baptism for the child in our day. "Strange as it might seem then," he writes,

> Paul the Apostle of the freedom of the Christian man from the bondage of legalism has turned out to be a catechist after the manner of a Rabbi. But instruction given in connection with baptism did not exhaust the paraenetical duties of the early Christian leaders, and Paul himself has expressly told us that he did not regard baptismal activity as his forte. He must have had many more things to teach his converts than could be pushed into a catechism at baptism. . . . The Church was for him, in Carrington's phrase, a "neo-levitical community"; and despite its freedom in the Spirit it had to know moral order also; it had to regulate its life. The Church, like every new sect within Judaism, had to draw up rules for the moral guidance of its members and had to define its position. Moreover, there is solid evidence that in doing this Paul and the other Christian leaders drew upon certain Jewish codes or regulations.[27]

In the light of Davies' observation, baptism seems to have been properly set within the context of education. The candidate was educated in terms of preparation for the baptismal event. The event itself was utilized for teaching purposes. Education, however, did not stop with the completion of this ceremony; baptism cannot encompass all that should be taught to a convert. It does appear, therefore, that the desired blend of grace, faith, ethics, and theology may be best assured by the conversion and ' baptism of a child at the time when he is yet spontaneous and receptive and before he has become the prisoner of a rigid legalism. Furthermore, Christian education and learning are just as appropriate after baptism as before it occurs.

It may be providential that, in practice, the churches of the believers' baptism category have largely denied their doctrinal position on this matter. They have been sheepishly performing what should

[27] W. D. Davies, *Paul and Rabbinic Judaism* (London: S.P.C.K. Press, 1958), pp. 129-130.

be an open practice. Instead of trying to fit the baptism of children into the stern haughtiness of the baptism of believers, we should ask ourselves whether or not this is necessary and justifiable. It does seem logical that baptizing a child old enough to make a personal response militates against the magic elements of infant baptism and the harsh legalism of the rite when administered to believers.

What about those people who have not grown up within the nurturing concern of the Church? These persons, as well as those who may have departed from the Christian community, in adolescence or later, cannot be placed in an identical category. Once again, we may take our cue from Judaeo-Christian history. The Church's mission to the outsider is akin to that of the responsibility of the early Church, comprised as it was of converted Jews, to the Gentiles of the period. Had these initial Christians realized their dependence upon God's grace, even when they were so busy with their "good works," Paul would have enjoyed a more pleasant relationship with the Jerusalem community. Furthermore, that community could have made a more effective witness to the world had it emphasized God's grace.

The exact opposite occurred, as Newbigin explains: "The Jews had thus misunderstood their position in relation to God and the Gentile world. They had not understood what the righteousness of God is. From the true premise that God had entered into a covenant with Abraham and his seed, they drew the false conclusion that if they kept their side of the covenant, they had a status before God as of right, from which the Gentiles were excluded." [28]

No wonder that Paul's emphasis was that baptism was into Christ. It seems evident that baptism into the early Jerusalem Church quickly took on the quality of a faith-work. Had the situation been otherwise, it could have been said with more authority that "the righteousness which alone is counted as righteousness in His sight, is simply that which casts itself in loving trust and gratitude upon His grace. . . ." [29]

The same situation persists. The grace of God is not an understood

[28] *Ibid.*, p. 44.
[29] *Ibid.*

need until the outsider stands in some degree of condemnation under the law. Recognition that he is unrighteous is a prerequisite to his ultimate conversion. Although this awareness may not be to the same degree as is found within the environment of the Church, man is not left without a covenant to refer to. It has been commonly supposed that Paul's reference, in the first two chapters of Romans, to the Gentile's knowledge of God and law was the result of his influence by the Stoics.

This would superficially explain such passages as: "For what can be known about God is plain to them, because God has shown it to them. Ever since the creation of the world his invisible nature, namely, his eternal power and deity, has been clearly perceived in the things that have been made. So they are without excuse. . . ." [30] A bit later Paul draws this conclusion: "When Gentiles who have not the law do by nature what the law requires, they are a law to themselves, even though they do not have the law. They show that what the law requires is written on their hearts, while their conscience also bears witness and their conflicting thoughts accuse or perhaps excuse them. . . ." [31]

Both passages reflect the Stoic's teaching that the knowledge of God was either a distinct element common to human nature or could be secured by observing the created order. While acknowledging Paul's debt to the Stoics, John Baille disagrees that this is the whole of the matter. "Nevertheless," he contends,

among these earlier covenants it was that made with the still undivided race after the Deluge, the so-called Noachic covenant, that appears to have been most appealed to in later Judaism. Such knowledge of God and of His laws as the heathen nations were observed to have was believed to be a relic of this original revelation. And this way of accounting for the knowledge of God which the Gentiles possess—a knowledge which, however overlaid and corrupted, is still sufficiently present in their minds to leave them

[30] Rom. 1:19-20.
[31] Rom. 2:14-15.

"without excuse"—is really much more germane to St. Paul's thought as a whole than the doctrine of Stoic origin which also influenced his writing at the beginning of the Roman epistle.[32]

Whether it be from within the Church or from outside the Church, a convert actually makes two confessions. When confronted with the covenanting God, whose law and/or righteousness he then affirms, man first confesses himself a sinner who turns away from unrighteousness unto righteousness. Perhaps no one ever becomes a Christian who does not first do this. If he learns this, he must learn it from the Jew; for this revelation came first to the Jew in our history. It is a healthy sign that there are voices in Jewish theology calling the Jews anew to this truth. One such is that of Arthur Cohen:

Theology is the enterprise by which a man seeks to understand his life in separation from and presentness before God. If it is his understanding of God's Word and teaching that he is to be obedient, he cannot but obey. If the way of obedience is the way of the commandments, he has no choice but to observe the commandments or run the risks of his disobedience. No man—not even a theologian—can pick and choose among the commandments. They are all the will of God, if indeed that will is expressed through Scripture and the tradition. But a man can— indeed he must—be faithful to conscience, even if it be a sinful and disobedient conscience. He cannot practice what he does not believe, even if his unbelief is the unbelief of pride and rebellion. But he can never—and this is where Reform Jewish theology is essentially wrong—excuse his disobedience by calling the Law obsolete, irrational or outmoded, or by confusing the commandments with preventive medicine, hygienics, or social and psychic therapy. There is disobedience in me and I confess it, not happily but truthfully, and I pray that God will countenance my disobedience and aid me through my unbelief. Such is the grace and mercy that I seek from God. But I have long since given up

[32] John Baille, *The Idea of Revelation in Recent Thought* (New York: Columbia University Press, 1956), p. 131.

any thought of rationalizing my unbelief or explaining my belief. It is all the Word of God and my willingness or refusal to hear it.[33]

The second confession must be either to the sin of self-righteousness in the law, or a cry for the gift of righteousness which man cannot secure by the law—not because the law is sinful but because he cannot do it. The child of the Church, while still a child, is not likely to be enmeshed in the sin of self-righteousness as is the case of an adult. If he is baptized into Christ at this time and remains true to the theology of that baptism, his witness to the world will be eminently enhanced. He has not been saved from the law as such. He has been saved from self-righteousness because God in Christ "has done what the law, weakened by the flesh, could not do . . ."[34]

5 Baptism and the Holy Spirit

Many temples of truth have fallen victim to the massive war against sacramentalism. It is hard to find the place of meeting between baptism and the Spirit among the ruins. Such a meeting place needs restoration.

Christian theology is generally agreed that the Spirit is the gift of the Risen Lord. There is no significant division on this point. How, when, and where the Spirit is manifestly given is another question. It has given rise to vigorous and prolonged debate.

The book of Acts suggests, in contradistinction to the weight of the New Testament, a chronological separation between the Holy Spirit and baptism. Pentecost, and later the conversion of Cornelius, locates the gift of the Holy Spirit before the event of baptism. On two other occasions the sequence is reversed wherein the Spirit follows in the wake of the ceremony.[35] These anomalies defy a facile explanation. A clue may be found in W. O. Carver's explana-

---

[33] Arthur A. Cohen, "A Theology of Jewish Existence," *The Christian Century*, January 23, 1963, p. 106.
[34] Rom. 8:3.
[35] Acts 8:14-17 and 19:2-7.

tion of Luke's purpose for the book. With the reminder that the common title, "The Acts of the Apostles," was missing from the earlier manuscripts and that the simpler "Acts" is not found before the fourth century, Carver continues:

> Only three of the Twelve are mentioned at all after the first chapter. It was not to tell the story of men, not even of apostles, that Luke wrote, not even of Peter, the great leader, nor of Paul, the mighty herald and teacher. He would rather show how the Holy Spirit carried forward the work Jesus began. In this work men are agents, but the Spirit is the power and the Mind. Luke selects for record those "acts" which reveal and illustrate the plan and method of the Holy Spirit. In this plan the full story of no man finds place. And he emphasizes results. At every section we find him eager to tell of believers won to the Lord.[36]

This is a plausible approach. It is possible that Luke's interest in the Spirit did not encompass the question as to how the Spirit was given. Acts may be somewhat remiss in connecting the Holy Spirit to Christ as well as to baptism. The work of the Spirit is described almost as an independent activity. The author was assuredly not occupied with the question of baptism and the Holy Spirit with any degree of consistency. This may be attested in his account of Philip's baptism of the eunuch. In that instance, the baptizer rather than the baptized is caught up by the Spirit.[37] We may assume, with some confidence, that Luke was more intent upon the Spirit's activity and achievements than interested in its origin, nature, or relationships.

As a result of these varied emphases, Christian theology has proposed that the Spirit is manifest in the dispensation of the Christian sacraments; that the Spirit illuminates, from within, the written Word to the "priesthood of believers"; and that the Spirit is in the individual person in whom it has come without ecclesiastical sanction or the biblical medium. In general, these are the theological reflections

[36] William Owen Carver, *The Acts of the Apostles* (Nashville, Tenn.: Broadman Press, 1916), p. 10.

[37] Acts 8:39.

of Roman Catholicism and Anglicanism, of Lutheran and Reformation doctrines, and of the sectarian thought of Anabaptists along with the several categories of Pietism.

Van Dusen casts a vote for the third segment; after observing that "the inward voice of the Holy Spirit takes precedence over the external word of scripture of the dicta of the prelate" (*vide* p. 127) he adds, "It is noteworthy that in the period, when the ecclesiastical idea had begun to overshadow all Christian thought, the belief in the Spirit tended to disappear, or to have a merely formal value. . . . The Spirit had meaning only so long as it acted directly on men as individuals, and when they could not receive it through the Church and its ordinances, they lost the feeling of its reality." [38]

Nonsacramental churches properly proclaim that the Spirit comes often to the person, without detours by way of church, sacrament, or sacred book. They fail to realize that in their rejection of the sacraments they forfeit the right to ask the question, "How does the Spirit come to the person?" If they attempt the answer—as they often do—that the Spirit comes by faith, ambiguity results. The question "how" is a query to which the free churches have no right, and it is bound to spawn a number of illegitimate answers. Consequently, these churches have sought to prove the Presence through a variety of talents and tongues. Paul's concern over the divisive influence of these proofs of the Spirit's visitation is well known to all and need not be labored at this point. There is every reason to believe that his doctrine of "baptism into one Spirit" was an endeavor to correct excessive display in which the Spirit seemed to have filled the human ego instead of the heart.

The two remaining questions, the when and where of the Spirit's coming, are rendered superfluous if "how" is asked and presumably answered. But these are pivotal questions for the position espoused here. It is not amiss to declare that the Spirit comes by faith if the believer objectifies the event in terms of time and place. He is not forced to say "how" if he has some sense of the "when" and "where." The absence of knowledge of these latter factors does not

---

[38] Henry P. Van Dusen, *Spirit, Son, and Father* (New York: Charles Scribner's Sons, 1958), p. 72.

dogmatically deny the reality of the Spirit's indwelling. But it can and often does mean that one's attempt to express the Presence becomes a subjective, divisive, unruly, and often arrogant endeavor.

Consider the baptism of Jesus. We may safely agree that "Never, with Jesus' baptismal experience before us, can we reverently say that 'nothing happens' in baptism. In Jesus' experience water-baptism proved to be Spirit-baptism, not only coincident in time but causally related: for the motives which brought Jesus to baptism were precisely those which made possible and inevitable the endowment of the Spirit. Henceforth, true baptism is inseparable from the gift of the Spirit: that is the measure of the change Christ's baptism wrought in biblical initiation." [39]

The causal relation between the baptism of Jesus by water and the baptism of the Spirit does not ascribe a sacramental value to the water or the act. The same Spirit which was the motivation for the baptism of Christ was the Spirit which descended upon Him at the event. The pertinent fact is that the Spirit was manifest when Christ identified Himself with man, as is so when man identifies Himself with Christ.

Although the coincidence in time between one's baptism and the gift of the Spirit cannot always be authenticated, they were coincident at the baptism of Jesus. The Scriptures record that the same was true with others who were baptized into Christ. On the other hand, attention has been called to passages which indicate that the Spirit visited the person sometimes before his baptism and sometimes afterward. This evidence is so unmistakably clear that it is foolish to disregard it. Despite this, it is impossible to separate baptism from the visitation of the Spirit. All evidence is agreed at one point. The Spirit does not prompt the person to circumvent baptism. If the Spirit comes before the event, the act is a certain consequence. If baptism precedes the Spirit's endowment, it is not authentic until the Spirit authenticates it. In the conversion of the individual, the one certain place of the meeting of the person and the Spirit is in baptism, even if the factor of the time element is uncertain.

[39] R. E. O. White, *The Biblical Doctrine of Initiation* (Grand Rapids, Mich.: Wm. B. Eerdmans Publishing Co., 1960), p. 98.

This is true because baptism is initiation into Christ.

> The New Testament begins by describing how the Holy Spirit
> descended upon Jesus and abode upon Him, and how in the
> Power of the Spirit He lived and spoke, and how the same Spirit
> was given to His Church to be the permanent principle of its
> life. . . . The Holy Spirit is now no more an occasional visitant
> to a favored individual, but the abiding and indwelling principle
> of life in a fellowship. The supreme gift of the Spirit is not the
> spectacular power by which an individual may gain pre-eminence,
> but the humble and self-effacing love by which the body is built up
> and knit together.[40]

One need not be happy with Newbigin's description of the Spirit
as a principle of the life of the Church and its fellowship in order
to agree that he has properly located the place of the Spirit. Not
only is this the usual dwelling of the Spirit, but it is the place into
which the Spirit leads the convert. He is baptized into Christ and
into His Spirit. For where Christ is, there also is His Spirit.

And if we ask the fundamental question, "How is Jesus present
to us today?" it is surely clear that at least a very central part of
the answer must be, "He is present in His people." [41] The relationship between baptism and the Presence is attested by the fact that
the Spirit knits together the body of Christ. Baptism is that body's
incorporation of the person into itself. Its reality is not only the
work of the body but the work of the Spirit. These truths provide
good soil for J. E. Fison's fine words: "It is not the eucharist and
the corporate parish communion or the individual faith of a revived
and deepened holiness that will provide the answer. It is only the
water and the Spirit. . . . It is therefore to holy baptism, the sacrament of the Spirit, that we must look for a right answer as to how
we . . . may regain contact with the living God. Only the Spirit can
make Christ our contemporary. Only the sacrament of the Spirit

[40] Lesslie Newbigin, *The Household of God* (New York: Friendship Press,
1954), p. 115.
[41] *Ibid.*, p. 50.

[baptism] can introduce us to the sacrament of the Lord [the supper]." [42]

As with Newbigin, the reader needs to distinguish between Fison's sacramentalism—the "how" of the Spirit's coming and dwelling—and his sense of the Spirit's work in baptism, regarding time and place. Nothing which has been said should imply that the act of baptism insures the presence and the work of the Spirit. Everything that has been said intends to persuade us that Christ, by His Spirit, has chosen the act of baptism as the time and place of the Presence for the purpose of bringing man into Christ—His death, burial, and resurrection. This we dare to say only if we remember that "the potency of baptism depends upon Christ who is the chief actor in it. It has no independent potency in itself. . . . Though the Church utters the Word in baptism and performs the act, what must always be believed in, loved, expected and prayed for is the power of His free person, sent down for this very purpose. It cannot be manipulated by man. It is always power which Christ Himself personally and freely grants. It is something promised which He Himself alone can provide." [43]

6   Baptism and the Church's Mission

The question of baptism is germane to the world mission of the Church. Baptism ought not only say something to the Church itself but also to the world. What it does say in both realms should avoid contradiction so that it does not give an "uncertain sound."

Some elements of the Church, defending the practice of infant baptism, have been forced to strange ideas about the Church and its mission. Without exception, so far as we know, they agree that either or both adult and believers' baptism is the only baptism available to the Church when it is in a missionary situation (*vide* pp. 36 f., 56 f.). Their defense of paedobaptism is based on the assumption that the Church has changed and that it no longer exists in a missionary

[42] J. E. Fison, *The Blessing of the Holy Spirit* (London, New York, Toronto: Longmans, Green & Co., Inc., 1950), p. 204.

[43] Karl Barth, *The Teaching of the Church Regarding Baptism,* trans. E. Payne (London: S.C.M. Press, 1945), p. 19.

situation akin to that of New Testament times. At the turn of the century, Forsyth concluded that the Church was no longer involved in a mission to a pagan world. He asserted that it had now reached the status of a "universal, settled and triumphant Church." [44]

By their own admission, paedobaptist theologians confess to the propriety and authenticity of adult baptisms whenever the Church is in a missionary situation—whenever it is engaged in a mission to the world. The possibility of exploiting this admission is an intriguing one. One must introduce two questions: Is it true that the Church is no longer in a missionary situation? In being true to its own nature, is there ever a time when the Church can be itself without being a mission?

It is incredible that anyone should now be saying that the Church is no longer in a missionary situation. It may not be a replica of that which obtained in New Testament times. But a studious look at the world today will not allow a place in our minds for an established and victorious Church with no place to go and no mission to live. The chilling labels "post-Christian man" and "post-Christian culture" should be enough to dispel any optimism that the Church is "universal, settled and triumphant."

The failure to read history properly is compounded by a misreading of the Church. Even if there were a time when the Church could not recognize its mission to the world, such as the period when Church and State were completely identified with each other, there was never a time when the Church was something other than a mission. Newbigin, although a paedobaptist, does not rob the Church of its mission as a means to defend his position. Not only does he find, as Bishop of the Church of South India, that the Church is in a missionary situation, but he also is convinced that the Church is always a mission. Speaking of the misunderstanding of the Church as a whole, he says: "The most obvious evidence is the fact that, in the thinking of the vast majority of Christians, the words 'Church' and 'mission' connote two different kinds of society. The one is conceived to be a society devoted to worship and the

[44] P. T. Forsyth, *Lectures on the Church and Sacraments* (London: Longmans, Green & Co., Ltd., 1917), p. 168.

spiritual care and nurture of its members. It is typically represented by a large and ancient building. The other is conceived to be a society devoted to the propagation of the Gospel, passing on its converts to the safe keeping of the Church." [45]

Churches that pride themselves by virtue of their missionary endeavors are not immune to Newbigin's discomforting spotlight. Often these churches have missions, not in grand edifices like their own, by which they reach out to the underprivileged, the differently colored, and ultimately to the "uttermost parts of the world." When a church sponsors what it calls a "mission church," this may only mean that it separates itself from its mission proper as a way of establishing "peaceful coexistence" between the strata of Christians. This is not the mission of Christ.

It is far better to say that the Church is a mission. The mission is not something which it possesses as one of its respectable characteristics. It is a mission or it is not a church! This view of the Church is not a supporting factor for the evangelistic endeavors of religious bodies so bent on a mission as to become something other than "church." Newbigin's further comment provides a balanced view:

> Precisely because the Church is here and now a real foretaste of heaven, she can be the witness and instrument of the kingdom of heaven. It is precisely because she is not merely instrumental that she can be instrumental. This is not merely theoretical matter, but one of real importance. There is a kind of missionary zeal which is forever seeking to win more proselytes but which does not spring from and lead back into a quality of life which seems intrinsically worth having in itself. If we answer the question, "Why should I become a Christian?" simply by saying, "In order to make others Christians," we are involved in an infinite regress.[46]

Within the Church there is a quality of life that needs no reason for being other than itself. Unbalanced missionary zeal provides, for

[45] Lesslie Newbigin, *The Household of God* (New York: Friendship Press, 1954), p. 164.
[46] *Ibid.*, p. 169.

those who look for it, a perfect excuse to keep undesirables out of their own local fellowship by providing for their conversion elsewhere. This is the unhappy explanation of the good conscience with which a southern church can spend mission funds in Africa while denying Negro membership in its local congregation. Missions, in this wise, are also contributing to race and class stratification at home as well as abroad.

"In other words, just as we must insist that a Church which has ceased to be a mission," Newbigin concludes, "has lost the essential character of a Church, so we must also say that a mission which is not at the same time truly a Church is not a true expression of the divine apostolate. An unchurchly mission is as much a monstrosity as an unmissionary Church." [47] Paedobaptist elements within the Church must accept their clear responsibility for building churches which are not missions. Defense of the doctrine and practice of baptism goes too far when it results in a misunderstanding not only of the world but also of the Church. Newbigin's vote for infant baptism in the light of what he believes about the Church is astonishing. We may thank him for his insight regarding the Church and continue to wonder at his unflagging support of infant baptism.

The world of the "lost" and unbelieving cannot comprehend all that is implicit in infant baptism. Not only is this so, but the child who grows up in the Church can have no sense of leaving one life for another if he merely joins, in a formal sense, that of which he is already an integral part. As has been suggested, Bushnell's protective concern that a child should never remember when he was not a Christian disregards a more vital factor. How can a Christian know what he has become and is, if he has no sense of what he was not? Our belief that the child is a proper subject for baptism must not in any way be construed to mean that his conversion should be a smooth, unconscious transition. The Church is the company of those who have become a new creation in Christ. It cannot say this to those of the outside world unless it is willing to say it first, and with equal vigor, to those who have belonged to its community and its tradition. Infant baptism is an obstacle to the church-mission in the

[47] *Ibid.*, p. 170.

missionary situation of today's world! Churches holding to its faith and practice must accept the responsibility for the barrier they have erected in the path of the Church—"going out and making disciples."

This is a relentless statement about infant baptism, and is so intended. Now, let it be said with equal vigor that rebaptism is not the answer. The first two reasons for this vigorous enjoinder against rebaptism are repetitions of positions already assumed in this book. Baptism, of any kind or form—proper or improper—must be accepted by all churches as the act of Christian initiation. Any interpretation to the contrary throws the meaning of baptism into a confused, dissipated state. Secondly, rebaptism, when baptism is understood as Christian initiation, can only indicate that the first baptism was not only invalid but that its subjects are not in the Church. No matter what devious explanations are offered in this context, rebaptism serves to unchurch a multitude of Christians.

A third reason, not heretofore mentioned, is decisive. The tension created by infant baptism for the Church in its world mission is the responsibility of paedobaptist churches. Consequently, in these institutions this tension must be reduced and the indicated correctives applied. Paedobaptist institutions must either be labeled as false churches because of infant baptism and its implications, or they must be confronted with correcting improper faith and practice within their own congregations and denominations. It is not possible for some Christian churches, by their action, to correct the improprieties of other Christian churches. Churches, with their locus in the tradition of believers' baptism, are justified in their criticism of infant baptism. They are not justified in their assumption that they can correct an error which has occurred outside the scope of their ministry.

Karl Barth is unequivocal on this point:

. . . the nature, power and meaning of baptism are fundamentally independent of the order and practice which are mutually conditioned by the Church and the person who is baptized. Let us set down at the outset everything that here [is] to be said, sued for and demanded as something half like a precaution: from first principles it is certain that no rejection of the order and practice of baptism through the fault of the Church, or through fault or lack on the part of the candidate, can make the baptism of a person, once it has been performed, ineffective and therefore invalid, or can lead to or justify a call to re-baptism according to a better order or practice. . . .

There is no kind of inadequacy in baptismal order and practice that cannot be removed or put right by means quite other than that of re-baptism. That may be written in advance of the remembrance book of Anabaptists of all kinds—Roman and those supposed to be evangelical. Nothing is going to be said in their favor.[48]

In the light of a former premise of his, one reacts to Barth's statement in different ways. He does not take seriously enough the inexchangeable nature of the symbol and the reality it represents. The "meaning" of baptism is not "fundamentally independent of the order and practice" in which it is enacted. If this were a fact, our concern for order and practice would be superfluous and ought to be eliminated. Barth is quite right, however, in his assertion that the correction of infant baptism, which is improper in both form and meaning, is not within the purview of those churches which are critical of it and do not practice it. The error of infant baptism can be corrected only by the Spirit which is the Power and Presence necessary to Christian baptism of any form. Rebaptism cannot escape the basic fallacy it deplores. It becomes a sacrament by presuming to be the only means by which the Spirit can perform its remedial task.

Paedobaptist institutions should retain the burden of responsibility for their own act in this regard. Rebaptism, while serving to heighten the tensions between the churches, unfortunately reduces the tension in which the entire question of baptism should remain. When the individual is rebaptized after having been baptized as an infant, he superficially fulfills an obligation for membership in the new congregation. Neither the individual nor his new fellowship show the

---

[48] Karl Barth, *The Teaching of the Church Regarding Baptism,* trans. E. Payne (London: S.C.M. Press, 1945), pp. 35-36.

intense concern called for in confronting the basic issues stemming from his baptism while still an infant. The tensions between the churches, intensified by rebaptism, should be reduced in order that the proper tension between the two extremes of baptism may be revived. This tension promises no fruitful resolution until local congregations are made up of members, holding equal privileges and responsibilities, who come from the two traditions. Associate membership is an evasion. It means nothing and can only result in second-class membership.

The last and most persuasive argument against rebaptism embraces the implications for the churches which practice it. This calls for yet another word about the Church as a mission and its connection with baptism. To what Newbigin has said, one may add the urgent statement of R. E. O. White.

> It seems enough to reply that the church is always facing a missionary situation, and that in any case it is in the missionary situation that she most clearly reveals the true nature of her gospel and strips down to its imperative essentials the form of her requirements. Advanced too often, this argument that the apostolic church stood in exceptional circumstances, so that apostolic teaching cannot be applied to later situations, must destroy altogether the relevance of New Testament studies to modern theological construction. "Primitive historical Christianity must always be essentially normative, and if later types of religion so diverge from the primitive type as to find the New Testament rather an embarrassment than an inspiration, the question they raise is whether they can any longer be recognized as Christian." [49]

A paedobaptist involved in the Church's mission offers an appropriate word about baptism in the missionary situation which White has underlined: "In missionary work today adult baptism is

[49] R. E. O. White, *The Biblical Doctrine of Initiation* (Grand Rapids, Mich.: Wm. B. Eerdmans Publishing Co., 1960), p. 178. Also, James B. Denny, *The Christian Doctrine of Reconciliation* (London: James Clark and Company, Ltd., 1959), pp. 27 f.

again in common use; and the forms here given have a missionary origin. . . . They were first written . . . under conditions similar in important respects to those in which the Church's baptismal rites originally took shape." [50]

The baptism of persons who make their personal faith-response to Christ's redemption is the proper baptism for the church mission. This is the consensus of all churches. Undeniably, the Church now finds itself in a missionary situation. Those churches that commonly demand rebaptism are the churches whose basic faith and practice in baptism are right for the Church's mission to the world. What then is the effect of rebaptism upon baptism as the symbol of the church-mission? Here is an impediment in the path of the mission of the Church which is equally as formidable as that of paedobaptist obstruction. Baptism cannot incorporate in two different ways. It cannot be the means by which the Church enrolls its converts from the world and, at the same time, be the means by which a Christian church enrolls a proselyte from another Christian church. Whenever this is practiced, the Church has forfeited the impact of its greatest and most forceful symbol to the world at large. That forfeiture occurs with churches that practice rebaptism. They unconsciously admit to this by deleting Christian initiation from the act or by reducing baptism to an inconsequential ordinance. Whenever the evangelistic church baptizes a recognized Christian from a recognized Christian church, it has made a mockery of its own baptismal faith and practice! It has completely distorted the missionary nature of believers' baptism. An inclusive missionary event has been changed into an exclusive, nonmissionary, "country club" bath!

As infant baptism is the responsibility of the churches practicing it, so rebaptism is the responsibility of those churches banning it. Its correction is also dependent upon the Spirit. The arena of that correction is circumscribed by the churches that need it. Paedobaptist institutions can no more correct the error of rebaptism than can the churches supporting believers' baptismal doctrine correct infant

[50] A. G. Hebert, *An Essay in Baptismal Revision* (London: Dacre Press, 1947), p. 5.

baptism. Each must look to what their baptisms do to the world mission as well as to what damage is wrought to the act of Christian baptism in its own right.

The reader must not presume this to be a plea for superficial ecumenicity. The prospect for realistic Christian unity has already been severely hampered by two undesirable ecumenical endeavors. Lay ecumenicity is much too provincial. It is the "church just around the corner" ecumenicity. The harassed mother is often heard to say, "One church is just as good as another. I want the children in Sunday school somewhere. So I think we will join the nice little church in the neighborhood. The children can walk to the activities."

On the other hand, the clergy is engaged in a new language. This "ecumenese," as one observer has dubbed it, is a neat semantic game. Played with caution, it goes like this: One clergyman says to another clergyman, "I think I think the way you think but you must speak first so that I will be sure to think the way you think." The ecumenical language is increasingly devoid of conflicting and controversial matter. This will ultimately result in speaking about nothing of consequence.

Clarence Tucker Craig's proposal, pertinent to this and related issues, is logical and attractive—so much so that one wonders why it has not received more attention. He pleads urgently that baptism be recognized as the rite of admission to the Church. So far as he is concerned, this ought to hold true with the baptism of infants and adults alike. "There can be no place for reception into the Church following the baptism of adults," he asserts. "All that can possibly remain is a pledge of loyalty to the particular part of the Church through which he has joined the Body of Christ. There is no way to join Christ's holy Church except as one joins some particular part. Let us hope that all our rituals will soon be made to conform at this point to sound theology." On these grounds, Craig logically suggests that "a pledge to support a particular church should be taken by anyone coming from another branch." [51]

[51] Clarence Tucker Craig, *The One Church* (Nashville, Tenn.: Abingdon-Cokesbury Press, 1951), p. 93.

Perhaps the obviousness of this practice has caused its disparagement by the theologians. If so, it is an unhappy situation. Within the scope of this approach, baptism does not lose the essential meaning of initiation. Rebaptism is seen in the bad light that it deserves. If it means Christian initiation, it presupposes that its subjects have neither been baptized nor have become members of the Church. If it stands as the means by which one joins with a local church of a particular denomination, it reduces baptism to a status far below that of Christian initiation. It is often described in this respect as the necessity by which one becomes a "Baptist."

At the same time, churches ought to retain their identity and demand theological conviction from their members by exacting some kind of tangible commitment from those persons who, crossing over denominational lines, join one church from another. This will keep alive the rich doctrinal diversity which owes its existence to the varied traditions within the church. If this diversity were lost by the imposition of surface unity, the hope for continuing theological concern and vitality in the coming days could hardly be justified.

Some churches could logically demand a commitment to their dogma and creed upon which they are doctrinally founded. Others may resort to an initiation by the means of a covenant relationship to which members, old and new, would give common allegiance. In the case of churches practicing local autonomy, new members of the category of which we speak could be granted the rights and privileges of full membership by the vote of the congregation in its church meetings.

There are many means, consonant with the churches' doctrines, by which members from other communions may be enrolled in new fellowships within the Church. Suffice it to say that any and all means to this end ought to be employed so that an artificial ecumenicity may be avoided. The one fundamental thing is that Christian baptism be saved from the status of being an expedient substitute for any of them.

Christians must make sure that Christian baptism becomes what it is intended to be.

7   A Reminder

The last chapter was not originally included in the scope of this book. It grew out of the insistent counsel and demand from a number of friends and colleagues. Their arguments could not reasonably be turned aside. A positive position, on the part of one who has tried to expose the façade behind which baptism has been practiced by the churches as a whole, became a matter of integrity.

This position, however right or wrong, is an honest one. In many instances it departs from the faith and practice of the congregations which I have served and the Southern Baptist Convention with which I have had long years of fellowship.

This explanation is offered, however, for a reason that is different from what the reader might suppose, on the basis of what is above. It is given as the means for reminding the reader that this book is mainly concerned with what his church in his tradition has done to baptism within its own faith and practice. It is at this point that we must begin to learn. All other roads are closed to us until we fulfill this obligation.

Index

Adoption, 52, 117
Ahlstrom, Sydney, 15
Allport, Gordon, 12(n), 22
Anabaptists, 55, 67-72, 81-87, 89, 96 f, 102, 127, 189, 197
Anderson, Oscar, 116 f
Argument from silence, 44, 176
Argyle, A. W., 49, 66

Baille, D. M., 54
Baille, John, 185 f
Bainton, Roland, 82 f
Baptism
  adult, 44, 115, 131
  believers, 9, 12, 18, 25, 35 f, 45, 50, 53, 55-57, 59, 63, 67, 77, 84, 92 f, 105, 120 f, 124, 126 f, 136, 141, 144, 152 f, 156 f, 176, 178, 181, 183 f
  confessional, 76
  dedicatory, 53 f
  infant, 9, 12, 18, 25, 35, 39 f, 42-44, 46 f, 49-53, 55, 57, 77, 87, 89, 95, 105 f, 108 f, 111-113, 115, 117, 120, 134, 151 f, 156 f, 176, 178 f, 184, 192
  into Christ, 61, 70, 165, 184
  John's, 41, 61 f
  mode, 73
  new testament, 43 f, 73, 89
  of Jesus, 61 f, 132, 190
  proselyte, 39-41, 47, 61, 65, 84
Baptists
  American, 73, 84
  educational literature, 141-145
  general, 69-73
  particular, 69-73, 83 f
  Southern, 9, 73, 84, 138

Barth, Karl, 74, 78, 98, 151, 192(n), 196 f
Beach, Waldo, 6
Bonhoeffer, Dietrich, 152
Broaddus, John A., 73
Brunner, Emil, 63 f, 148, 155, 166 f, 170 f, 176 f
Bushnell, Horace, 118, 133-136, 139-143, 195

Calvin, John, 41, 52-54, 71, 86-89, 117
Carver, W. O., 187 f
Casuistry, 21-24
Catechism, 46 f, 183
Christian education, 10, 30, 105, 132-148, 181
Christian initiation, 5, 28, 33, 81-83, 89-91, 103, 164-169
Church
  and state, 4, 82, 98, 193
  Anglican, 71, 83 f, 89-92, 108, 189
  Congregational, 118 f
  Disciples of Christ, 68, 111
  Episcopal, *see* Anglican
  established, 51, 70, 157
  Latter Day Saints, 153
  Lutheran, 116 f
  Methodist, 111-116
  mission, 192-198
  missionary situation, 36 f, 50
  of England, *see* Anglican
  Presbyterian, 87 f, 119 f
  Roman Catholic, 8, 23, 68, 94 f, 99-103
Church, Leslie, 115
Circumcision, 39-42, 47, 115

205